Islam and Terrorism

by Mark A. Gabriel

Charisma®
HOUSE

ISLAM AND TERRORISM by Mark A. Gabriel
Published by Charisma House
A part of Strang Communications Company
600 Rinehart Road
Lake Mary, Florida 32746
www.charismahouse.com

Unless otherwise noted, all Scripture quotations are from the Holy Bible, New International Version. Copyright © 1973, 1978, 1984, International Bible Society. Used by permission.

Scripture quotations marked KJV are from the King James Version of the Bible.

Quotations from the Quran marked "Ali translation" are from *The Quran Translation,* 7th edition, by Abdullah Yusef Ali (Elmhurst, NY: Tahrike Tarsile Quran, Inc., 2001).

Quotations from the Quran marked *"The Noble Quran"* are from *The Noble Quran,* English Translation of the Meanings and Commentary published by King Fahd of Saudi Arabia in Medina, "The City of Light," Saudi Arabia in 1998. The translators were Dr. Muhammad Taqi-ud-Din Al-Hilali and Dr. Muhammad Muhsin Khan.

Library of Congress Catalog Card Number: 2002100697
International Standard Book Number: 0-88419-884-7

03 04 05 06 — 9 8 7 6 5
Printed in the United States of America

Dedication

I dedicate my book to Kamil and Elsa,
my spiritual parents, for their love
and for caring and looking after me
during my years in South Africa.
They showed me true Christianity.

Acknowledgments

I am so thankful for the help I have received from:

The family of Charisma House

My friend who translated the manuscript
from Arabic to English

The patient editor who did a wonderful job with
the English manuscript

The leadership of Florida Christian University,
who greatly encouraged me as I wrote this book

This book will radically change your view of the religion of Islam, not only because the author was a devout Muslim for most of his life, but also because he was a well-educated Muslim clergyman whose reputation was spotless. I have personally interviewed the author and checked his references, and I can vouch for the veracity of his story.

—Dr. Robert A. Morey, Executive Director
Research and Education Foundation

This book, *Islam and Terrorism*, should be read by everyone. As a graduate of Princeton Theological Seminary and dean of a university with a subsidiary seminary, I knew some of the information in this book. But I had trouble believing that Islam really is so committed to destroying Christians and all non-Islamic governments. The author, Dr. Mark Gabriel, clearly documents the identification between modern terrorism and Islamic theology. He also explains his journey to Christian faith and the resultant persecution by family and country. I was especially impressed by his explanation regarding the "love for Christians" passages in the Quran. He explained that they are from earlier, weaker Mecca years, and that in the later years at Medina, when the prophet had total control, retribution was proclaimed. Muslims call this distinction *naskh*—that the later words of retribution for infidels replaced the previous words of love. This book is a must-read for everyone striving to understand the roots of terrorism in the world today and the conflict with Islam.

—Rev. Bruce H. Yurich, Ph.D.
Dean of Florida Christian University

Contents

Foreword by J. Lee Grady. ix

Introduction xiii

Section I
My Story

1   Disillusioned at Al-Azhar 1

2   The Egyptian Prison 7

3   A Year Without Faith. 13

Section II
The Roots of Terrorism in Islam

4   Core Beliefs of Islam 23

5   Holy War in the Quran 33

6   Misinformed by the Media 41

7   Human Rights Under Islam 51

Section III
Following Muhammad's Example

8   Arabian Culture. 65

9   Muhammad Declares Jihad 69

10 The Ultimate Goal of Islam 81

11 The Three Stages of Jihad 85

12 When Lies Are Justified. 91

13 Muhammad's Use of Mosques 97

SECTION IV
THE DEVELOPMENT OF MODERN JIHAD

14 Forefathers of Terrorism 103

15 The Founding Father of Modern Jihad 113

16 The Philosophers of Jihad 123

17 Recruiting for Holy War 133

18 Inspired by Iran 139

19 Treachery Between Terrorists 143

20 Al-Jihad Prepares and Attacks 151

21 Justice Loses, Quran Wins 157

22 Jihad Bleeds Out of Egypt 167

23 New Strategy: Attack the West 175

SECTION V
MUSLIMS AND THE GOOD NEWS

24 The False Christianity Presented to Muslims . . 187

25 Bringing the Gospel to Muslims 195

26 Challenges for Muslim Converts 203

   Epilogue 215

   Notes 221

   Glossary 227

   Bibliography 233

Foreword

THERE IS SOMETHING that God is saying loud and clear through the tragedy of September 11, 2001. We have more than a billion people on this planet who are followers of the religion of Islam, and the church of Jesus Christ must respond in taking our faith to those people.

The problem is that we have such limited understanding of what Muslims believe and who they are. And it's not helpful when you turn on the television and hear people saying that Islam is the answer to America because it has such great family values, which is what some Muslims said on *Oprah* shortly after the attack.

It is confusing for us when we hear different signals. Our president and other government leaders make statements like, "Islam is a peaceful religion." But then we hear other leaders say that Islam is not a peaceful religion. A debate is going on: What is true Islam? Is it what the Muslim clerics in the United States are saying? Or is it what the Muslim clerics in Afghanistan or Pakistan say?

In the chapters that follow, you will read a remarkable

discussion of the roots of terrorism that have been at the core of Islam since the prophet Muhammad received the first verses of the Quran in about A.D. 610. These roots are traced from Muhammad all the way to the present day.

What makes this book so special is that it is written by a former professor of Islamic history at the most prestigious Islamic university in the world. The books you buy at your local bookstore about Islam and terrorism are written by Americans—American journalists, American politicians, ex-CIA officials and so on. Dr. Gabriel offers a point of view you will never hear from them—the point of view of one who lived Islam, studied Islam, taught Islam and preached Islam at mosques in the Middle East. This is a scholar who earned both master's and doctorate degrees in Islamic study.

This is a man who nearly lost his life more than once at the hands of Islamic radicals. His body shows the scars, and he tells that story in the beginning of this book.

Dr. Gabriel reveals historical facts about Muhammad's teaching and practices that few Westerners have ever heard. He shows, in fact, that Islamic fundamentalists today are practicing Islam just as Muhammad did.

He explains the development of terrorism during the past few decades from the point of view of one living in the Middle East. He identifies the key philosophers and tells you about the contents of books that are so dangerous they have been banned by Middle Eastern governments and their authors put to death. These books can only be obtained on the black market, but their ideas are fueling the fires of terrorism.

He explains the religious basis behind radical actions. Why would someone be willing to vaporize himself in a jet crash in the name of Allah? The answer lies in a system of belief that is full of works but lacking in hope.

Some facts are unsettling—this is a powerful evil at loose in the world—but the overall message brings a strong sense of peace. All the disjointed events we see on the news make sense when viewed through the framework of Islamic fundamentalism. Behind the physical battle, the spiritual battle is now visible.

Dr. Gabriel reminds us, "Islam is behind terrorism, not Muslims. Muslims are victims. Even the nineteen young people who hijacked the planes and were killed in the crashes—they are victims. The criminal is Islam."

Dr. Gabriel has a vision of hope for the future. Just as Islam has an agenda for world domination, God has an agenda to bring salvation to as many as possible, including those trapped in Islam.

—J. LEE GRADY
EDITOR, *CHARISMA* MAGAZINE

Introduction

THE NAME YOU see on the cover of this book is not the Muslim name that was given to me by my parents in Egypt. However, I would like to say that I have no desire to deceive Muslims, Christians or anyone else about my name in order to benefit myself. Rather, I have chosen to change my name for the following reasons.

Reason #1

After I left Egypt, I went to South Africa and was discipled in Christ there. When I began ministering to Muslims in South Africa, I became very well known by my Muslim name. For four years radical Muslims pursued me diligently. I had to hide all the time and change my residency from one city to another almost on a monthly basis. When I wrote my first book in South Africa, my pastor and I discussed whether I should put my name on it. We decided to change my name for security reasons.

Reason #2

I was not comfortable living my Christianity by a Muslim name. I felt my Muslim name was part of my old man. When a person called me by that name, it reminded me of my old life. I want to live by a Christian name.

Choice of name

I chose the first name of Mark because Mark was a writer of the Gospels. Mark was also the first Christian who went to Egypt with the Good News. When Jesus sent the seventy out from Jerusalem, Mark brought the gospel to the city of Alexandria in Egypt.

I chose the last name of Gabriel because Gabriel was the angel who brought the good news of the coming of the Messiah to the virgin Mary. Also this was the name of the first Christian person I met in South Africa who took me into his home and invited me to his church.

REFERENCES TO THE QURAN

The Quran, which is Islam's holy book, is divided into 114 chapters called *surahs*. The surahs are also divided into verses, like in the Bible. If you have a copy of the Quran, you can look up passages using the surah and verse numbers. Muslims often refer to the chapters by their chapter name, but I have not included these with every reference because they are of limited significance to the Western reader.

I have used two different English translations of the Quran. One is the version translated by Abdullah Yusef Ali. The other I will refer to as *The Noble Quran*. This was published and printed by the king of Saudi Arabia in 1998. This translation is similar to *The Amplified Bible* in the sense that it expands and clarifies the meaning of the text through comments in parentheses and brackets.

You should be aware, however, that the English translations sometimes do not accurately reflect the original Arabic, particularly when the passage would be offensive to Westerners.

Here is an example to give you an idea of what I am talking about. Surah 8:39 is a very key verse regarding those who reject the Quran, yet the following translation is quite vague:

> And fight them on until there is no more tumult or oppression, and there prevail justice and faith in Allah altogether and everywhere.
>
> —ALI TRANSLATION

The Noble Quran is a bit more straightforward.

> Fight them until there is no more *Fitnah* (disbelief and
> polytheism, i.e. worshipping others besides Allah) and
> the religion (worship) will be for Allah Alone [in the
> whole of the world].

HELPS FOR READING THIS BOOK

There are times when I refer to "the prophet Muhammad,"
meaning the founder of Islam. I use the word *prophet* to dis-
tinguish him from the many other Muhammads in the
Islamic world.

I have been told that Arabic names are often difficult for
Western readers. Here are a few tips that will help you as
you read:

- When you see a *q*, it is pronounced like the *k* in
  kite.

- When you see two consonants next to each other,
  the word is pronounced with a very short vowel
  sound between those consonants. For example,
  ibn would be pronounced "ib-in"; *Qutb* would be
  pronounced "kutib," in one syllable.

- The words *bin*, *ibn* and *bn* mean "son of." The
  word *al* means "the."

To help you keep track of names and other key concepts, I
have included a glossary in the back of the book.

Many of the books I have used as sources were obtained
outside of the United States and are written in Arabic. Some
are available only on the black market, but I have given the
most complete publication information that I can.

I have included photos of the key people who developed the philosophy of terrorism that is being practiced by fundamentalists today. These pictures were collected from various Arabic books.

Also, to make it easier for Western readers to visualize the geographic places mentioned, the publisher has included a map of the Islamic world. (See page 165.)

FOCUS ON RELIGIOUS TERRORISM

The focus of this book will be religious terrorism, also known as *jihad*, or holy war, in Islam. The reason I call it religious terrorism is because it is done in the name of Islam and to establish a religious agenda.

Because we are looking specifically at terrorism, there are many details about Islamic history and Islamic faith that I have not mentioned because they are not pertinent to the focus.

SECTION I
MY STORY

Chapter 1

Disillusioned at
Al-Azhar

FIFTEEN YEARS AGO I was the imam of a mosque in the city of Giza, Egypt, which is where the famous Egyptian pyramids are located. (Imam of a mosque is a position similar to pastor of a Christian church.) I preached the message of the week on Fridays from 12 to 1 in the afternoon, as well as performed other duties.

One Friday the topic of my message was jihad. I told the two hundred fifty people seated on the ground before me:

> Jihad in Islam is defending the Islamic nation and Islam against the attacks of the enemies. Islam is a religion of peace and only will fight against one who fights it. These infidels, heathens, perverts, Christians and Allah's grievers, the Jews, out of envy of peaceful Islam and its prophet—they spread the myth that Islam is promulgated by the sword and violence. These infidels, the accusers of Islam, do not acknowledge Allah's words.

At this point I quoted from the Quran:

> And do not kill anyone whose killing Allah has for-
> bidden, except for a just cause.
> —SURAH 17:33, *THE NOBLE QURAN*

When I spoke these words, I was just freshly graduated from Al-Azhar University in Cairo, Egypt—the oldest and most prestigious Islamic university in the world. It serves as the spiritual authority for Islam worldwide. I was teaching at the university, and I was an imam on the weekends at this mosque.

I preached my sermon on jihad that day according to the philosophy of the Egyptian government. Al-Azhar University focused us on the politically correct Islam and purposely overlooked areas of teaching that conflicted with the authority of Egypt.

I was preaching what they taught me, but inside I was confused about the truth of Islam. If I wanted to keep my job and my status at Al-Azhar, however, I needed to keep my thoughts to myself. After all, I knew what happened to people who differed from Al-Azhar's agenda. They would be fired and would not be accepted to teach at any other university in the nation.

I knew that what I was teaching at the mosque and at Al-Azhar was not what I'd seen in the Quran, which I had memorized in its entirety by the age of twelve. What confused me the most was that I was told to preach about an Islam of love, kindness and forgiveness. At the same time, Muslim fundamentalists—the ones who were supposed to be practicing true Islam—were bombing churches and killing Christians.

At this time the jihad movement was very active in Egypt. Reports of bombings and attacks against Christians were common. It was such a part of everyday life that one time I heard a bomb go off at a church as I was riding the bus. I looked and saw a plume of smoke rising up a quarter mile away.

I had been raised in a family that was well established in Islam, and I had studied Islamic history. I was not involved in any radical groups, but one of my Muslim friends was a member of an Islamic group that was actively slaughtering Christians. Ironically, he was a chemistry student and had only recently become serious about his faith. Nevertheless, he was active in jihad. One day I asked him, "Why are you killing our neighbors and countrymen whom we grew up with?"

He was angry and astonished at my challenge. "Out of all Muslims you should know. The Christians did not accept the call of Islam, and they are not willing to pay us the *jizyah* (tax) to have the right to practice their beliefs. Therefore, the only option they have is the sword of Islamic law."

SEEKING THE TRUTH

My conversations with him drove me to pour over the Quran and the books of the Islamic law, hoping to find something to contradict what he said. I couldn't change the reality of what I read.

As a Muslim, I realized I had two options:

- I could continue to embrace the "Christianized" Islam—the Islam of peace, love, forgiveness and compassion, the Islam tailor-made to fit Egyptian government, politics and culture—thereby keeping my job and status.

- I could become a member of the Islamic movement and embrace Islam according to the Quran and the teachings of Muhammad. Muhammad said, "I left you with something [the Quran]. If you hold on to what I left with you, you will not be led astray forever."[1]

Many times I tried to rationalize the kind of Islam I was practicing by saying to myself, *Well, you are not too far out. After all, there are verses in the Quran about love, peace, forgiveness and compassion. You only need to ignore the part about jihad and the killing of the non-Muslims.*

I went to every interpretation of the Quran trying to avoid jihad and killing non-Muslims, yet I kept finding support of the practice. The scholars agreed that Muslims should enforce jihad on infidels (those who reject Islam) and renegades (those who leave Islam). Yet jihad was not in harmony with other verses that spoke of living at peace with others.

All the contradictions in the Quran were really causing a problem for my faith. I spent four years to earn my bachelor's degree, graduating second out of a class of six thousand. Then there was another four years for my master's and three more for my doctorate—all studying Islam. I knew the teachings well.

In one place alcohol was forbidden; in another it was allowed. (Compare Surah 5:90–91 with Surah 47:15.) In one place the Quran says Christians are very good people who love and worship one God, so you may be friends with them (Surah 2:62, 3:113–114). Then you find other verses that say Christians must convert, pay tax or be killed by the sword (Surah 9:29).

The scholars had theological solutions to these problems, but I wondered how Allah, almighty and all powerful, could either contradict himself so much or change his mind so much.

Even the prophet of Islam, Muhammad, practiced his faith in ways that contradicted the Quran. The Quran said Muhammad was sent to show the mercy of God to the world. But he became a military dictator, attacking, killing and taking plunder to finance his empire. How is that showing mercy?

Allah, the god revealed in the Quran, is not a loving father. It says that he desires to lead people astray (Surah 6:39, 126). He does not help those who are led astray by him (Surah 30:29) and desires to use them to populate hell (Surah 32:13).

Islam is full of discrimination—against women, against non-Muslims, against Christians and most especially against Jews. Hatred is built into the religion.

The history of Islam, which was my special area of study, could only be characterized as a river of blood.

DANGEROUS QUESTIONS

Finally, I reached the point where I was questioning the faith and the Quran with my students at the university. Some of them were members of terrorist movements, and they were enraged: "You can't accuse Islam. What has happened to you? You have to teach us. You have to agree to Islam."

The university heard about it, and I was called in for a meeting in December 1991. To summarize the meeting, I told them what was in my heart: "I can no longer say that the Quran comes directly from heaven or from Allah. This cannot be the revelation of the true God."

These were very blasphemous words in their opinion. They spat in my face. One man cursed me, "You blasphemer! You bastard!" The university fired me and called the Egyptian secret police.

THE SECRET POLICE KIDNAP ME

To understand what happened next, you need to have a picture of how my family lived. My father had a very large home that was three stories tall. My whole family lived together in this house—my parents, my four married brothers with their families, my unmarried brother and myself. Only my sister lived elsewhere because she was married and lived with her husband.

The house was divided into many apartments, and we were very comfortable. On the first floor were my parents' apartment and an apartment I shared with my brother. On the floors above us were apartments for my other brothers.

At three o'clock in the morning on the very same day that the university kicked me out, my father heard knocking at the door of our house. When he opened the door, fifteen to twenty men rushed in carrying Russian Kalashnikov assault weapons. They were not wearing uniforms, just regular clothes. They ran upstairs and all through the house, waking people up and looking for me. I think so many men came in at once so that I couldn't run away before they found me.

They were all over the house before one of them found me asleep in my bed. My parents, brothers, spouses and children were awake, weeping and terrified, as the men dragged me away. Everybody in the area heard the commotion.

I was taken to a place that looked like a prison and was placed in a cell. In the morning my parents frantically tried to figure out what had happened to me. Right away they went to the police station and demanded, "Where is our son?" But nobody knew anything about me.

I was in the hands of the Egyptian secret police.

The Egyptian Prison

S PENDING TIME WITH the Egyptian secret police is very different from a visit to an American prison. They put me in a cell with two radical Muslims accused of committing terrorist acts. One was Palestinian, and the other was Egyptian.

For three days I was given no food or water.

Every day the Egyptian man asked me, "Why are you here?" I refused to answer because I was afraid he would kill me if he knew that I had questioned Islam. On the third day, I told him I was a teacher at Al-Azhar University and an imam in Giza. Immediately he gave me a plastic bottle of water and some falafel and pita that were brought to him by his visitors, but he told me that the police had warned him not to give me anything.

On the fourth day, the interrogation began. For the next four days the goal of the secret police was to make me confess that I had left Islam and to explain how it happened.

The interrogation began in a room with a large desk. My interrogator sat behind the desk, and I sat on the other side.

Behind me were two or three police officers.

They were sure that I had been evangelized and converted to Christianity, so the interrogator kept badgering me, "What pastor did you talk to? What church have you been visiting? Why have you betrayed Islam?"

He asked many questions. One time I hesitated too long when I answered. He nodded to the men behind me. They grabbed my hand and held it down on the desk. My interrogator held a lit cigarette. He reached over and extinguished it into the top of my hand. I still have this scar. I also have the scar on my lip where he did the same thing. Sometimes he used the cigarettes when he got angry; other times the officers just hit me across my face.

As my interrogation continued, the pressure grew stronger. One time they brought a fire poker into the room (the iron rod that you use to move burning wood in a fire). I wondered, *What is that for?* The next time the interrogator wanted to make his point, I found out. The poker was red-hot, and one officer pressed it into the flesh of my left arm.

They wanted me to confess that I had been converted, but I said, "I didn't betray Islam. I just said what I believe. I am an academic person. I am a thinker. I have a right to discuss any subject of Islam. This is part of my job and part of any academic life. I could not even dream of converting from Islam—it is my blood, my culture, my language, my family, my life. But if you accuse me of converting from Islam for what I say to you, then take me out of Islam. I don't mind to be out of Islam."

THE WHIP

My answer was not what they wanted to hear. I was taken to a room with a steel bed in it. They tied my feet to the foot of the bed and then put heavy stockings, almost like oven mitts, on them.

One officer had a black whip, about four feet long, and he began whipping my feet. Another officer sat down next to me at the head of the bed with a pillow in his hands. When I cried out, he pushed the pillow into my face until I was quiet. I could not stop crying out, so a second officer came to put an extra pillow over my face.

As I was beaten I became unconscious, but when I woke up the officer was still whipping my feet. Then he stopped and they untied me, and one officer commanded, "Stand up." I couldn't at first, but he took the whip and beat my back until I stood.

Then he showed me a long passageway and said, "Run." Again, when I couldn't do it, he whipped my back until I ran down the passageway. When I got to the end, there was another officer waiting for me. He whipped me until I ran back to where I came from. They made me run back and forth.

Later, I learned why they did that. The running was so that my feet wouldn't swell. The stockings were so I wouldn't have marks on my feet from the whipping. I assume the pillows were so nobody could hear my cries.

Next I was taken to something that looked like a small, aboveground swimming pool. It was filled with ice-cold water. The officer with the whip said, "Get in," so I got in. It was so cold that I tried to get out, but he whipped me every time I made a move.

I have low blood sugar, and it wasn't very long before I passed out from the cold. When I woke up I was lying on my back in the bed where they whipped my feet, still in my wet clothes.

A NIGHT IN THE DARK

One evening I was taken outside behind the building. I saw what looked like a small, concrete room with no windows or doors. The only opening was a skylight on the roof. They made me climb a ladder to the top and demanded, "Get in." When I sat on the edge and put my feet down in the opening, I felt water. I could also see there was something swimming on the top of the water. *This is my grave*, I thought. *They are going to kill me today.*

I slid down the opening and felt the water rise up over my body, but then to my surprise I felt solid ground under my feet. The water only came up to my shoulders. Then rats, which were what I saw swimming in the water, started crawling all over my head and face. These rats had not been fed for a very long time. My interrogators were being clever. "This guy is a Muslim thinker," they said, "so we will have the rats eat his head."

I was very scared for the first minute after they closed the skylight. They left me there all night and then came back the next morning to see if I was alive. When the skylight opened and I saw the sunlight, it was hope for me that I had survived and was still alive.

All that night not one rat bit me. They climbed all over my head and in my hair and played with my ears. One rat stood on my shoulders. I felt their mouths against my face, but it almost felt like kisses. I never felt a tooth. The rats were utterly faithful to me.

Even today when I see a rat, I have a feeling of respect. I cannot explain why the rats behaved this way.

MEETING WITH A DEAR FRIEND

The interrogation was not over. Later the officers took me to the door of a small room and said, "There is someone who loves you very much who wants to meet with you."

I asked, "Who is this?" I was hoping it was one of my family members or a friend to visit me or get me out of prison.

They said, "You don't know him, but he knows you." They opened the door to the room, and inside I saw a big dog. There was nothing else in the room. Two people took me inside and then left me and shut the door.

This was the first time my heart cried out. In my heart I cried to my Creator, *You are my father, my God. You are to look after me. How can You leave me in these evil hands? I don't know what these people are trying to do to me, but I know You will be with me, and one day I will see You and meet You.*

I walked to the middle of the empty room and slowly sat down cross-legged on the floor. The dog came and sat down in front of me. Minutes went by as this dog looked me over. I watched his eyes move from top to bottom over and over again. I prayed in my heart to the God I did not yet know.

The dog got up and started walking in circles around me, like an animal about to eat something. Then he came to my right side and licked my ear with his tongue. He sat down by my right side and just stayed there. I was so exhausted. After he just sat there, I fell asleep.

When I woke up, the dog was in the corner of the room. He ran to me, as if to say good morning. Then he licked my right ear again and sat down again at my right side.

When the officers opened the door they saw me praying

with the dog sitting next to me. I heard one say, "I can't believe this man is a human being. This man is a devil—he's Satan."

The other replied, "I don't believe that. There is unseen power standing behind this man and protecting him."

"Which power? This man is an infidel. It's got to be Satan because this man is against Allah."

SOMEONE WATCHING OVER ME

They took me back to my cell. While I was gone, my Egyptian cellmate had asked the police, "Why are you persecuting this man?"

They told him, "Because he is denying Islam." That made my cellmate furious. As soon as I got back in the cell, he was ready to kill me. But I had only been in there fifteen to twenty minutes when a police officer came with transfer papers for this man and took him away.

I had to ask myself, *What is going on here? What power is protecting me?* At that time, I did not know the answer.

I did not spend much time wondering about it. In a short while my own transfer papers came through. I was to be taken to a permanent prison in southern Cairo.

At this point I did not think that my interrogators were even human. I had been arrested for merely questioning Islam. Now my faith was really shaken. And I was on my way to another prison.

Chapter 3

A Year Without Faith

HE NEXT WEEK I spent in a prison in southern Cairo. It was a relatively relaxed time. God sent me a prison guard who did not agree with radical Islam.

All during this time my family was trying to find out where I was. They had no success until my mother's brother, who was a high-ranking member of the Egyptian Parliament, returned to the country after traveling overseas. My mother called him, sobbing, "For two weeks we have not known where our son is. He is gone." My uncle had the connections that were needed. Fifteen days after I was kidnapped, he came to the prison personally with the release papers and took me home.

Later, the police gave my father this report:

> We have received a fax from Al-Azhar University accusing your son of leaving Islam, but after an interrogation of fifteen days, we found no evidence to support it.

My father was relieved to hear this. Out of all my brothers and sisters, I was the only one who had studied Islam at the university, and he was very proud of me. He could not even imagine I would ever leave Islam, so he attributed the whole incident to a bad attitude toward my scholarship on the part of the people at the university.

"We don't need them," he said, and he asked me to start work immediately as a sales director for his factory. He owned a successful business that produced leather jackets and men's and women's clothing.

A YEAR WITHOUT FAITH

For one year I lived without any faith. I had no God to pray to, to call to or to live for. I believed in the existence of a God who was merciful and righteous, but I had no idea who He was. Was He the God of the Muslims, the Christians or the Jews? Or was He some animal—like the cow of the Hindus? I had no knowledge of how to find Him.

You have to understand that if a Muslim comes to the conclusion that Islam is not the truth and he has no religion to turn to, it is the most difficult time in his life. Faith is in the fabric of the life of a Middle Eastern person. He cannot imagine how to live without knowing his God.

During this whole year, my physical body expressed the pain that was in my spirit. Though I had every material thing I needed, I was plagued with a deep tiredness from constantly trying to use my mind to figure out the identity of the true God. I suffered constantly from headaches. I went to a doctor who was a relative of the family. He did a scan of my brain, but he did not find anything wrong. He prescribed some tablets that helped.

THE SERMON ON THE MOUNT

I ended up visiting a nearby pharmacy one or two times a

week for packets of tablets, getting a small number of tablets each time, hoping the headaches would just go away for good. After I had been coming for a while, the pharmacist asked me, "What is going on in your life?"

I told her, "Nothing is going on. I have no complaint except for one thing: I am living without God. I don't know who my God is or who created me and created the universe."

She said, "But you were a professor at the most respected Islamic university in Egypt. Your family is very respected in the community."

"That is true," I replied, "but I have discovered falsehoods in their teachings. I no longer believe my home and family are built on a foundation of truth. I had always clothed myself in the lies of Islam. Now I feel naked. How can I fill the emptiness in my heart? Please help me."

"OK," she said. "Today I will give you these tablets, and I will give you this book—the Bible. But please promise me not to take any tablets before you read something from this book."

I took the book home and opened it at random. My eyes fell on Matthew 5:38:

> You have heard that it was said, "Eye for eye, and tooth for tooth." But I tell you, Do not resist an evil person. If someone strikes you on the right cheek, turn to him the other also.

My whole body began trembling. I had studied the Quran my whole life—not once did I find words as inspiring as this. I had come face to face with the Lord Jesus Christ.

I lost all track of time. It felt as if I were sitting on a cloud above a hill, and in front of me was the greatest teacher in the universe telling me about the secrets of heaven and the heart of God.

I could easily compare the Bible to what I had learned from my years of studying the Quran, and there was no doubt in my mind that I was finally encountering the true God. I was still reading in the early hours of the next day, and by dawn I gave my heart to Jesus.

AMBUSHED

I told only the pharmacist and her husband that I had accepted Jesus, but in Egypt, if anyone left Islam, it was automatically assumed that he had become a Christian and therefore must be killed. Because of this, fundamentalists sent two men to ambush me and kill me.

It happened when I was walking home from visiting a friend. It was only a fifteen- or twenty-minute walk through Giza. I was on Tersae Street, near my home, when I saw two men standing in front of a grocery shop. They were dressed traditionally with the long, white robes, long beards and head coverings. I thought they were just customers. I never imagined they would do anything to me.

When I reached the shop, they stopped me, and then suddenly both pulled out knives and began trying to stab me. I had no weapon, and because it was a hot day, I was just wearing a T-shirt and pants. I put up my hands to protect myself. Again and again the blades struck me and cut my wrists.

There were other people on the street, but no one helped me. They just gathered to watch. This was typical for those years. People would intervene if it was just a fistfight, but they wouldn't get involved with knives. They also didn't want to be in the way if someone pulled a gun.

The first attacker was trying to stab my heart. He almost did it, but I moved. He missed by about five inches and got me in the shoulder instead. When he pulled the knife out,

I remember looking down and seeing the blood come out in a stream.

I fell to the ground and just curled up in a little ball, trying to protect myself. Then the other attacker tried to stab me in the stomach, but the blade turned, and he stabbed me in the shin instead.

By this time I had lost so much blood that I passed out. There was no hope for me until two police officers arrived on motorcycles and my attackers ran away.

I was taken to the hospital and treated. In the hospital, the police asked if I knew why I was attacked. I said I did not.

Again, my father rejected any evidence that I was abandoning Islam. He just could not think in those terms.

MY FATHER LEARNS THE TRUTH

I continued to work for my father and did not speak of my new faith. In fact, he sent me to South Africa in 1994 to explore business opportunities for him. While there, I spent three days with a Christian family from India. When we parted, they gave me a small cross on a necklace to wear. This small cross marked the turning point in my life.

After a little more than a week, my father noticed the chain on my neck and became very upset because, according to Islamic culture, only women are allowed to wear jewelry around their necks. "Why do you wear this chain?" he demanded.

It seemed as if my tongue spoke on its own as I replied, "Father, this is not a chain. This is a cross. It represents Jesus, who died on a cross like this for me, for you and for everybody in the whole world. I received Jesus as my God and Savior, and I pray for you and for the rest of my family to also accept Jesus Christ as your Savior."

First, my father fainted right there in the street. Some of my brothers rushed out to him, and my mother started crying in fear. I stayed with them as they bathed my father's face with water. When he came to, he was so upset he could hardly speak, but he pointed at me. In a voice hoarse with rage he cried out, "Your brother is a convert. I must kill him today!"

Wherever he went, my father carried a gun under his arm on a leather strap. (Most wealthy people in Egypt carry guns.) He pulled out his gun and pointed it at me. I started running down the street, and as I dove around a corner, I heard the bullets whining past me. I kept running for my life.

LEAVING MY HOME FOREVER

I ran to my sister's house, which was about half a mile away. I asked her to help me get my passport, clothes and other documents from my father's house. She wanted to know what was wrong, and I told her, "Father wants to kill me." She wanted to know why, and I said, "I don't know. You must ask Father."

When I ran away, my father knew exactly where I was headed because my sister and I were very close, and her house was nearby. My father had walked to my sister's house, and he arrived while she and I were talking. He banged on the door, crying with tears streaming down his face, "My daughter, please open the door." Then he shouted, "Your brother is a convert! He has left the Islamic faith. I must kill him now!"

My sister opened the door and tried to calm him down. "Father, he is not here. Maybe he went to another place. Why don't you go home and relax, and later we can talk about this as a family."

My sister had mercy on me and gathered my things from

my parents' house. She and my mother gave me some money, and I got in my car and drove away on the evening of August 28, 1994.

For three months I struggled to travel through Northern Egypt, Libya, Chad and Cameroon. I finally stopped in the Congo. At that point I had malaria. They found an Egyptian doctor to examine me. He said that I would be dead by morning, and they made arrangements to get a coffin from Congo's Egyptian embassy to send me back home.

To their shock, I woke up the next morning. I left the hospital after five days and started to tell people everywhere about what Jesus did for me.

LIFE AS A FOLLOWER OF JESUS

Ten years have gone by since I accepted the Lord Jesus as my Savior. He called me and gave me a personal relationship with Him—something that Islam never offered.

I have never stopped crying for my Muslim people, whom I left behind, asking the Lord to deliver them from the darkness of Islam.

As you read the pages of this book, you will come to understand how great this darkness is. It is the teachings of Islam that have produced terrorists who seem capable of any kind of evil in the name of Allah.

Now the whole world wants to understand what Islam teaches. A great amount of misinformation has been shared in the media and on the Internet. My goal is to help you see plainly why these people do what they do.

I don't want to motivate you to anger, however. I want to motivate you to believe—to believe for the fall of Islam and the release of its captives, in Jesus' name.

Section II
The Roots of Terrorism in Islam

Chapter 4

Core Beliefs of Islam

The Mind-Set of Violence

W HEN I WAS a freshman at Al-Azhar University in 1980, I enrolled in class called Quranic Interpretation. Two times a month we would gather to hear lectures from a blind sheikh whose passion for Islam made him popular among the students.

Yet his radical side was obvious. Anytime he encountered a reference in the Quran to Christians or Jews, he took great delight in referring to the Christians as "infidels" and Jews as "the children of pigs." He made it clear that he wanted to bring back the glory days of the Islamic empire through jihad.

One day he gave us students an opportunity to ask questions. I stood up and asked him something I had been wondering about for a long time: "Why is it that you teach us all the time about jihad? What about the other verses in the Quran that talk about peace, love and forgiveness?"

Immediately his face turned red. I could see his anger, but I could also see that he chose to control it. Instead of yelling at me, he took the chance to reinforce his position in front of the five hundred students who were listening. "My brother," he said, "there is a whole surah [chapter] called 'Spoils of War.' There is no surah called 'Peace.' Jihad and killing are the head of Islam. If you take them out, you cut off the head of Islam."

Today that man is locked up in a prison in the United States. His name is Omar Abdel Rahman, and he was convicted of masterminding the first bomb attack of the World Trade Center, which occurred in 1993.

Before he came to America, he was the spiritual leader of the radical Egyptian group al-Jihad, which carried out the assassination of Egyptian President Anwar Sadat. Later in this book I will tell the incredible story of how Sheikh Abdel Rahman talked the Egyptian Supreme Court into setting him free, which gave him the ability to travel to the United States and practice jihad there.

ISLAM 202

As you can see from this story and from my testimony, I have lived close to terrorism for most of my lifetime. People in the West have a hard time understanding terrorists. They wonder, *Are they just all crazy?*

I can assure you, these people are not lunatics. Nor are they psychopaths who find psychological pleasure in hurting others. No, they are following a philosophy, and once you understand this philosophy, none of their actions will even surprise you.

In this chapter I will tell you the basics of Islam, but we are going to move beyond that very quickly in order to explain the specific religious doctrine that motivates an Islamic terrorist. I will also explain how fundamentalists do away with the verses in the Quran that speak of living in peace and harmony.

Submitting to Allah

The word *Islam* means "submission"; the word *Muslim* means "one who submits to Allah." The Quran says you cannot be a true Muslim unless you submit.

> O you who believe! Obey Allah and obey the Messenger (Muhammad) and those of you (Muslims) who are in authority.
>
> —Surah 4:59, *The Noble Quran*

Now, the question you must answer when submitting to Allah is, What does Allah want? The answer is found in the holy books of Islam—the Quran and the hadith.

The Quran was started in A.D. 610 when Muhammad, the prophet of Islam, said the angel Gabriel spoke to him while he was meditating in a cave near Mecca. Muhammad claimed these were the words of the one true god—Allah. Muhammad wrote down these words as he received them over a period of about twenty-two years. In short, the Quran is not Muhammad's teachings; it is Allah's words. It is significant that the revelations did not all come at the same time, as we will see later.

The books of hadith are another set of holy writings. These are books that record a verified account of things the prophet Muhammad said and did during his life. In other words, the books of hadith give the teachings of Muhammad in word and example.

Here's how the books of hadith were created. People who were close to Muhammad, such as his friends or wives, observed and recorded his activities. Scholars collected these writings and put them into the six sets of books that we now have. They are referred to by the editor of the books, i.e., hadith by Sahih Al-Bukhari.

The majority of the Muslim world considers hadith to be authoritative. (To be specific, Sunni Muslims accept it all; Shiite Muslims accept most. For example, the Shiites reject the thousands of hadith recorded by the second wife of Muhammad.)

Again, you need to be aware of hadith because Muhammad's life and teachings have served to establish principles of warfare and coercion that are practiced today. I will describe these facts in more detail later.

Finally, you need to be aware of the *Sharia*, which is the Islamic law regarding the duty of Muslims toward the God of Islam. *Qutb al-Fiqh* is the word used for the books that describe Islamic law. These are not specific books, like the books of hadith. These books are a whole body of literature, some ancient and some modern.

A RELIGION BASED ON WORKS

So, what does the Quran and hadith tell us that Allah wants? There are five key requirements that must be met in order to be a Muslim. These requirements are known as the five "pillars of Islam."

1. *Statement of belief.* There must be acceptance of the Muslim statement of faith: "There is no god but Allah, and Muhammad is his prophet."

2. *Prayer.* Muslims are to pray five times a day while facing Mecca, the birthplace of Muhammad. Prayers are at dawn, afternoon, late afternoon, after sunset and night. Special prayers are on Fridays.

3. *Giving alms.* This is similar to a tax. It is paid at

the end of the year and distributed to those in need.

4. *Fasting.* Fasting takes place during the Islamic month of Ramadan, which begins in middle November. During this fast, Muslims do not eat or drink during daylight hours. A light meal and a large amount of water are taken in before daybreak. After the sun sets, a heavier meal is eaten, and a large amount of liquid is consumed.

5. *Pilgrimage.* Muslims are encouraged to make a pilgrimage at least once in their lifetimes to Mecca where a five-day ritual is followed.[1]

Why is it so important that Muslims do what Allah wants? It's because Islam is a religion of works. Entrance to Paradise (heaven) must be earned. The sad part is that Muslims can never have assurance of salvation. When they die, they believe that they go to the grave, where they await their judgment at resurrection day.

When judgment day comes, Allah weighs the good works and the bad works and decides their fate.

> Then as for him whose balance (of good deeds) will be heavy, he will live a pleasant life (in Paradise). But as for him whose balance (of good deeds) will be light, he will have his home in *Hawiyah* (pit, i.e., Hell).
> —SURAH 101:6–9, *THE NOBLE QURAN*

There is no guarantee of Paradise even if you do good works all your life. It all depends on what Allah decides.

GUARANTEED ENTRANCE TO PARADISE

There is only one way to guarantee entrance into Paradise—and this makes the perfect motive for suicide bombers and jihad fighters. The only way to know for sure that you will get into Paradise is to die in jihad—to die while fighting the enemy of Islam.

Jihad simply means that Muslims must fight the enemy of Allah until the enemies die or the Muslims die. The word *jihad* actually means "struggle." Jihad has even been defined in legal terms by Islamic *fiqh* as follows:

> [Jihad] is fighting anybody who stands in the way of spreading Islam. Or fighting anyone who refuses to enter into Islam (based on Surah 8:39).

If you die in jihad, you don't even have to go to the grave and wait for judgment; you go directly to Paradise.

Jihad is really a contract between Allah and the Muslim. If the Muslim fights, Allah rewards him in the afterlife.

> Let those (believers) who sell the life of this world for the Hereafter fight in the Cause of Allah, and whoso fights in the Cause of Allah, and is killed or gets victory, We shall bestow on him a great reward.
> —SURAH 4:74, *THE NOBLE QURAN*

In reference to those who fight jihad, the Quran also says:

> For them Allah has got ready Gardens (Paradise) under which rivers flow, to dwell therein forever. That is the supreme success.
> —SURAH 9:89, *THE NOBLE QURAN*

When a person dies in jihad, a different burial procedure is followed. After a regular person dies, his body is washed and dressed nicely, as if going to the mosque. When a person dies in jihad, his body is not washed or given clean clothes. That person goes into the coffin just as he died. The blood is a witness for him in front of Allah—a sign of honor. Muslims believe the angels will treat him as a special person to Allah.

Western media have poked fun at the Muslim understanding of Paradise (heaven)—virgins for men to enjoy and so forth—but it is much more significant to recognize that dying in jihad is the only way a Muslim can be assured of entering Paradise at all. This is why you see Muslims leaving their own nations to fight jihad in other countries. Their motivation is religious, which is much more dangerous than a political motivation.

Jihad is definitely commanded for all Muslims in the Quran, but right now let's answer an important question many people ask: What about all the "nice" verses in the Quran?

"But What About . . . "

You have probably heard on television or read in the print media about verses in the Quran that speak positively about Christians or verses that encourage kindness. You may have wondered, "Are those verses really there?"

Here is the solution to the mystery: The Quran is filled with contradictions. You can find verses where Christians are complimented as well as verses where Christians are condemned to hell.

There are contradictions about other subjects as well. For example, there was much drinking of alcohol in Arabian society during Muhammad's day. One revelation told Arabs to stop drinking alcohol when going to mosque for prayer, but when prayers were finished they could resume drinking. Later another verse came and prohibited alcohol all the time.

(Compare Surah 2:219 and Surah 5:90.)

Another example is the relationship between Muslims and Christians. Some verses say that Muslims can have a good relationship with Christians, but other verses say Muslims must require Christians to convert to Islam.

In the beginning of Islam, the women were not forced to wear a *hijab*, but in subsequent verses, women were commanded to stay in the house and wear a cover.

Islamic scholars had to determine, therefore, which verses to follow in the case of a contradiction. This was accomplished by the principle of *naskh*.

Naskh is based on the fact that the Quran was revealed to Muhammad at different times over a period of about twenty-two years. Some parts of the Quran came later, and some parts came earlier. To solve a contradiction, they decided that new revelations would override (*nasikh*) previous revelations.

There are at least 114 verses in the Quran that speak of love, peace and forgiveness, especially in the surah titled "The Heifer" (Surah 2:62, 109). But when Surah 9:5 was revealed later, it canceled out those previous verses. This verse states:

> Fight and slay the Pagans wherever you find them, and seize them, beleaguer them, and lie in wait for them in every strategem (of war); but if they repent, and establish regular prayers and practise regular charity, then open the way for them: for Allah is Oft-forgiving, Most Merciful.
>
> —ALI TRANSLATION

This is known as the verse of the sword, and it explains that Muslims must fight anyone who chooses not to convert to Islam, whether they are inside or outside of Arabia. It is considered to represent the final development of jihad in Islam.[2]

The principle of *naskh* is very strong. If a verse is *nasikh*, or overridden, it is as if that verse doesn't even exist.

You might ask, "Why are there contradictions in the Quran in the first place? Why did the revelations change over time?" That question can be answered by looking at the life of Muhammad, the prophet of Islam.

At first the messages that were revealed to Muhammad were peaceful and kind in order to attract people. But circumstances changed.

Muhammad encountered much opposition in Mecca, the city where he first preached his message, so he left in A.D. 622. He went to Yathrib, a city now known as Medina, and built up military strength and a larger number of followers. (Both Mecca and Medina are located in present-day Saudi Arabia.) When Muhammad was in a position of power, he was able to return and conquer Mecca and surrounding areas. This move changed Islam from a spiritual religion to a political revolution.

The prophet Muhammad's life in Mecca was all about prayers and meditation, so the Quranic revelations in Mecca talk about peace and cooperation with others. But in Medina, Muhammad became a military leader and invader, so the revelations in Medina talk about military power and invasion in the name of Islam (jihad).

Sixty percent of the Quranic verses talk about jihad, which stands to reason because Muhammad received most of the Quran after he left Mecca. Jihad became the basic power and driving force of Islam.

It would be nice if the surahs in the Quran were organized in the order that they were revealed, but they are not. Some versions of the Quran will identify each verse as to whether it was revealed in Mecca or Medina; however, you must go to more scholarly references to know the exact order of the revelations.

SUMMARY

In this chapter you have learned some very necessary concepts that will help you to understand the mind-set of an Islamic terrorist. In summary:

- Islam requires submission to Allah, whose words are written in the Quran.

- On Judgment Day, Allah weighs your good and bad works and decides whether you go to Paradise or hell.

- Allah stated in the Quran that if you die in jihad, then you are spared judgment and automatically go to Paradise.

- The verses in the Quran that speak of jihad override (*nasikh*) the verses that speak of love and kindness.

- Jihad is the motivation behind almost every act of terrorism that is done in the name of Islam.

The Quran gives a great deal of practical teaching on the subject of jihad because it was so much a part of Muhammad's life in Medina. The next chapter will give Quranic verses about practicing jihad and address the question of whether all Muslims believe this.

Chapter 5

Holy War in the Quran

Fighting Unbelievers Until They Are Subdued

W E FIND JIHAD as a command to all Muslims enforced by the Quran. The focus of jihad is to overcome people who do not accept Islam. In Muhammad's day, jihad was therefore practiced against Christians and Jews on a regular basis, as well as people who were idol worshipers—anyone who did not convert to Islam. (See Surah 2:217; 4:71–104; 8:24–36, 39–65.) Let's let the Quran speak for itself.

> Those who reject Islam must be killed. If they turn back (from Islam), take (hold of) them and kill them wherever you find them...
> —SURAH 4:89, *THE NOBLE QURAN*

> So, when you meet (in fight—*Jihad* in Allah's Cause) those who disbelieve, smite (their) necks till when you have killed and wounded many of them, then bind a bond firmly (on them, i.e. take them as captives).
> —SURAH 47:4, *THE NOBLE QURAN*

> O you who believe! Fight those of the disbelievers who
> are close to you, and let them find harshness in you;
> and know that Allah is with those who are *Al-*
> *Muttaqun* (the pious).
> —SURAH 9:123, *THE NOBLE QURAN*

Allah commanded the prophet Muhammad to enforce
killing rather than taking prisoners.

> It is not for a Prophet that he should have prisoners of
> war (and free them with ransom) until he had made a
> great slaughter (among his enemies) in the land.
> —SURAH 8:67, *THE NOBLE QURAN*

Muslims were told to prepare themselves to fight against
the unbelievers.

> Let not the Unbelievers think that they can get the
> better (of the godly): they will never frustrate them.
> Against them make ready your strength to the utmost
> of your power, including steeds of war, to strike terror
> into (the hearts of) the enemies, of Allah and your ene-
> mies, and others besides, whom you may not know,
> but whom Allah knows.
> —SURAH 8:59–60, ALI TRANSLATION

JEWS AND CHRISTIANS ARE ENEMIES OF ISLAM

In the Quran, Christians and Jews are called the "People of the
Book" in reference to the Scriptures that they follow. At first,
the Quranic revelations encouraged Muslims to live at peace
with Christians. (The revelations about Jews were never posi-
tive.) But after Muhammad's move to Medina, the revelations
regarding all "People of the Book" became very hostile.

The following verse is considered to be the final revelation from Allah regarding Christians and Jews; therefore, it is understood to override all other revelations. It states:

> And fight them until there is no more *Fitnah* (disbelief and polytheism, i.e., worshipping others besides Allah) and the religion (worship) will all be for Allah Alone [in the whole of the world]. But if they cease (worshipping others besides Allah), then certainly, Allah is All-Seer of what they do.
>
> —SURAH 8:39, *THE NOBLE QURAN*

In other words, this verse says, "Fight those who reject Islam until all the worship is for Allah alone." The Quran also says Muslims must not be friends with Christians or Jews.

> Take not the Jews and the Christians as *Auliya* (friends, protectors, helpers), they are but *Auliya* of each other. And if any amongst you takes them (as *Auliya*), then surely he is one of them.
>
> —SURAH 5:51

This fact is also emphasized in Surah 5:52–57 and Surah 4:89. When fighting Christians, the Quran says to punish them severely so they will leave their homes and be dispersed (Surah 8:57).

The Quran commands Muslims to force Christians and Jews to convert to Islam with very strong and direct words. The following is from *The Noble Quran* in English, which includes commentary in the parentheses.

> O you who have been given the Scripture (Jews and Christians)! Believe in what We have revealed (to Muhammad) confirming what is (already) with you, before We efface faces (by making them like the back of

necks; without nose, mouth, eyes) and turn them hind-
wards, or curse them as We cursed the Sabbath-breakers.
And the commandment of Allah is always executed.

—SURAH 4:47

Just in case the meaning is not crystal clear, this translation
has a footnote at the bottom of the page, which reads, "This
Verse is a severe warning to the Jews and Christians, and an
absolute obligation that they must believe in Allah's
Messenger Muhammad and in his Message of Islamic
Monotheism and in this Quran."

CONVINCING THE MUSLIMS TO GO FIGHT

When you read these Quranic verses, it is helpful to think of
them in their historical context. Allah told Muhammad to go
out and conquer the world, so many Quranic verses were
given that encouraged the people to fight jihad. Here are
some examples:

> Allah has preferred in grades those who strive hard
> and fight with their wealth and their lives above those
> who sit (at home). Unto each, Allah has promised
> good (Paradise), but Allah has preferred those who
> strive hard and fight above those who sit (at home) by
> a huge reward.
>
> —SURAH 4:95, *THE NOBLE QURAN*

Those who did not participate in jihad were threatened
with hell fire.

> . . . they hated to strive and fight, with their goods and
> their persons, in the cause of Allah: they said, "Do not
> go forth in the heat." Say, "The fire of Hell is fiercer in
> heat." If only they could understand!
>
> —SURAH 9:81, ALI TRANSLATION

Those who retreat would incur Allah's wrath.

> If any do turn his back to them on such a day—unless it
> be in a stratagem of war, or to retreat to a troop (of his
> own)—he draws on himself the wrath of Allah, and his
> abode is Hell—an evil refuge (indeed)!
> —SURAH 8:16, ALI TRANSLATION

Obviously, you can see that killing, or jihad, is not an
option. It is a must because it is Allah's command (Surah
9:29). Every Muslim must do it to fulfill his faith. The only
exceptions are those who are disabled, blind and crippled
(Surah 4:95)

ISLAM'S ULTIMATE GOAL

Jihad is carried out in order to achieve the ultimate goal of
Islam—to establish Islamic authority over the whole world.
Islam is not just a religion; it is a government, too. That is
why it always gets down to politics. Islam teaches that Allah
is the only authority; therefore, political systems must be
based on Allah's teaching and nothing else.

The Quran states:

> If any do fail to judge by (the light of) what Allah has
> revealed, they are (no better than) Unbelievers . . . If
> they fail to judge by (the light of) what Allah has
> revealed, they are (no better than) those who rebel.
> —SURAH 5:44, 47, ALI TRANSLATION

People fighting jihad consider themselves to have succeeded when a nation declares Islam as both their religion
and their form of government. Nations where this has been
accomplished include Afghanistan (under the Taliban), Iran
(through Ayatollah Khomeini's revolution) and Sudan

(under Hasan al-Turabi). Islamic fundamentalists are actively working to gain control of the "secular" Muslim governments of Algeria, Egypt, Syria, Turkey, Palestine, Iraq, Lebanon, Saudi Arabia, Libya, Malaysia and others.

Man-made political systems—from democracies to dictatorships—are considered invalid. Moderate Muslims, however, do not always agree with this. A good example is past Egyptian president Anwar Sadat. He pronounced that there would be "no politics in Islam and no Islam in politics."

This statement was unacceptable to my former university professor Sheikh Omar Abdel Rahman, who had become the spiritual leader of the Egyptian terrorist organization al-Jihad. After President Sadat said those words, Sheikh Abdel Rahman declared that the president was an infidel renegade who should be killed. Following Islamic law, al-Jihad carried out the declaration of its leader and shot the president to death. President Sadat paid the ultimate price—his life—in an effort to stop Islam from becoming the governing authority in Egypt in the 1980s.

In the 1980s radical Islamic groups focused their attacks on their own governments. Now these organizations are turning to attack the West directly. Later in this book I will explain why.

DO ALL MUSLIMS REALLY BELIEVE THIS?

This is a very good question. At this point, Westerners may be wondering if their Muslim neighbors are a part of a plot to overthrow their government. To answer this question, we must recognize that there are different kinds of Muslims, just as there are different kinds of Christians.

The secular Muslims

This is a good description of Muslims all over the world. They believe in the nice parts of Islam, but they reject the call to jihad. They take on the cultural trappings of the message, but they are not living it out completely. These Muslims may be very dedicated to their system of thought, even though it does not represent true Islam. The majority of Muslims around the world—both in the East and in the West—fall into this category.

The traditional Muslims

There are two types of traditional Muslims.

The first type includes people who study Islam, know it and practice it, but they have a stumbling block with the concept of jihad. Some consider jihad to be a spiritual battle, like the Muslim Sufism movement.

The second type includes people who know that jihad is fighting non-Muslims, but they do not take action because 1) they do not have the ability to do it by themselves, 2) they are concerned about what would happen to their lives, family and children if they join a fundamentalist group, or 3) they want to live a nice life on earth instead of dying.

The fundamentalist Muslims

These are the ones who perpetrate terrorism. They sometimes have the long beards and head coverings. Their goal is to practice Islam as Muhammad did. Though we call them radicals, they are practicing true Islam.

NOW YOU KNOW THE BASICS

Now you know the key facts of Islam. In contrast, let's look at what the media have been telling us.

Misinformed
by the Media

Making Islam Look Good to the West

ONE OF THE indirect results of the events of September 11, 2001, was a wave of attention in the media regarding Islam. Islam was almost always represented as a religion of peace. It was made to be palatable to the Western ears.

The experts who were interviewed tried to separate the religious side of Islam from its political side, which cannot be done. When you see a Muslim on TV or print media saying that Islam is a religion of peace, it can be explained one of two ways:

1. *Wishful thinking.* Although this is not the Islam taught in the Quran, this person really wishes that it were. He sincerely believes he can explain away the unpalatable parts.

2. *Deceit with the intent to attract converts.* This is jihad practiced a different way. Instead of killing the enemy, you convert them with lies.

WISHFUL THINKING

An excellent example of wishful thinking about Islam is the show aired by popular talk-show host Oprah Winfrey. "Islam 101" aired on October 5, 2001–after the attack against America but before the U.S. took action in Afghanistan.

Oprah had a few Muslim guests on the show to educate the audience about the basics of Islam. One of the show's guests that day was thirty-one-year-old Queen Rania, the modern, Westernized queen of Jordan. Oprah asked her to comment on whether women in Islam were equal to men.

First of all, asking Queen Rania about anything in Islam is like asking Michael Jackson about his Christianity and what the Bible really teaches. Nevertheless, the queen and the other Muslim women on the show acted as if they were the highest authorities on Islam. With great conviction, the queen stated, "Islam views women as full and equal partners to men, so [women's] rights are guaranteed by Islam."[1]

Her answers made Western viewers feel good, but they do not accurately reflect the teachings of the Quran regarding women. If women are equal to men, why does the Quran say:

1. A Muslim man can be married to four women at the same time, but a Muslim woman can only be married to one man. "Marry (other) women of your choice, two or three, or four" (Surah 4:3, *The Noble Quran*).

2. Men have the right to ask for a divorce, but not women (Surah 2:229).

3. Women only inherit half of what men inherit (Surah 4:11).

4. Women may not serve as imams, and they are not allowed to lead prayer in the presence of men. (Man must always be above woman according to Surah 4:34.)

5. A woman is not allowed to answer the door at home if her husband is not there, even if it's her brother or a relative at the door. (This is derived from Surah 33:53, where Muhammad was giving instructions to people who visited his home. He said that if he wasn't home, they had to speak to his wives through a screen.)

6. Women should stay in their houses (Surah 33:33). Many Muslim women cannot travel without the permission of their fathers or husbands.

7. If a wife refuses to have sexual relations with her husband, it is permissible for the husband to physically beat her until she submits (Surah 4:34).

8. During jihad, when a man dies, he goes to heaven and Allah rewards him with incredible energy to enjoy sex with seventy virgins the first night. What happens if a woman dies in jihad? What is her reward—to be one of the seventy?

I am not sure whom the queen was trying to convince—herself or the world. The prophet Muhammad once said, "A cheap rug is more valuable in a man's home than a woman."[2]

Oprah also questioned Queen Rania about the veil (*hijab*) that some Muslim women wear. The queen said, "It's a personal choice. Some people are more conservative than others." She pointed out that she herself chooses not to wear one.[3]

About the issue of the veil in Islam, the following are the Quranic verses that command women to cover themselves.

> O Prophet! Tell your wives and your daughters and the women of the believers to draw their cloaks (veils) all over their bodies (i.e. screen themselves completely except the eyes or one eye to see that way).
> —SURAH 33:59, *THE NOBLE QURAN*

> And stay in your houses, and do not display yourselves like that of the times of ignorance...
> —SURAH 33:33, *THE NOBLE QURAN*

The only people allowed to see a woman's face are her husband, children, siblings and parents:

> It is no sin on them (the Prophet's wives, if they appear unveiled) before their fathers, or their sons, or their brothers, or their brother's sons, or the sons of their sisters, or their own (believing) women, or their (female) slaves.
> —SURAH 33:55, *THE NOBLE QURAN*

Islamic law has generalized these instructions to Muhammad's wives to apply to all women. (See Surah 24:31.) Queen Rania and other wishful thinkers like her do not recognize that they cannot interpret the Quran to suit their own preferences.

Oprah Winfrey's show was just another opportunity for these Muslim women to present the secular, Westernized, compromised and Christianized Islam that is not supported by the Quran and Islamic teaching. I hope that Oprah will find out the truth about Islam and present the correct information to her audience on this subject.

DECEIT

During one of my visits to the United States in August of 1998, I was staying with a family friend near Los Angeles. As we were surfing through TV channels, an Islamic program caught our attention. To my amazement, I heard the announcer say, "In a minute we will enjoy a spiritual journey through the prophet Muhammad's life with Brother Paul."

I did not move from the television set until I saw Brother Paul. I almost hit the floor when I laid eyes on him. He was a dark man with black hair and a thick, long, black beard, and he was wearing a long white robe and a tiny little head covering. Paul probably graduated from some Islamic institute in the Middle East and came to the United States as a missionary to spread Islam in the West.

I'm thinking, *Paul? Paul is a Muslim name now? This guy is 100 percent Middle East Muslim who grew up just like me. There is no way that is his real name.* What flabbergasted me was how Brother Paul used familiar Christian lingo like, "The Lord bless you; the grace of our Lord be with you; God bless you." He talked about God the Creator and how mankind can have a relationship with Him, how we can hear His voice and He can hear our prayers, and that we should allow the Spirit of God to work in us.

My head was spinning listening to this program that was broadcast from California. I was thinking, *Now I understand how they are spreading Islam in the U.S. and Europe.* I jumped out of my seat and cried out, "O God, have mercy on America! God, protect America and Your people in this great country. Please expose this great deception! Rescue this nation from this great deception!"

My friend and his family tried to comfort me by saying,

"God's protective hand has been on America since day one, and it will always be."

I asked my friend, "Why is this man lying to Americans about his name? Why would he present to America a new Islam that is totally different from the one that I grew up experiencing for most of my life? Why would he present an Islam that is much closer to Christianity than to the real Islam that I studied for so many years?" I told my friend, "This man should tell America his real name. Most likely it is Muhammad, Ahmed, Mahmoud, Mustaffa, Omar or Osama—not Paul."

This was the first time that I witnessed Muslims presenting a totally new Islam to the West. The average Muslim from the Middle East would never recognize it as the Islam that he practiced.

It is now obvious that many Islamic leaders are doing their part for jihad by influencing the Western media. Yes, they are doing their part when they fool the majority by getting them to believe that Islam is not for killing; that it is only a religion, not a political system; and that it is for peace, love, forgiveness and so on. That will keep Islam the fastest-growing religion in the world. It is just a different practice of the same principles of jihad.

Remember, Muslims declared jihad worldwide, but every Muslim is playing by different rules. One is using guns and bombs, and another is using words and lies to increase the numbers of Muslims worldwide. The method makes no difference; they are both sincere Muslims and it is one jihad according to the Quran—jihad against the enemies of Allah who resist the spread of Islam worldwide.

What amazes me is the audacity of these people. They hung the American flag over their centers, schools, mosques and Islamic institutes. They posted signs saying, "God Bless America" or "United We Stand." In the meantime, their fellow Muslims in the Middle East were burning American flags and posting signs supporting bin Laden and his act of terrorism on America.

In all fairness, some "wishful thinking" Muslims really did support America at this time. But other Muslims were doing what was simply expedient at the moment. They are a good example of Islamic politics in non-Islamic lands. These Muslims will lie and say things they do not believe at any moment as long as doing so would help Islam. Their loyalty is to Islam, not to the nation where they are living.

NATIONAL LOYALTY

I know that many people will disagree with me by saying, "There are many American and European Muslims who are loyal and sincere to their countries. After all, these countries have been their homes for many years." I would like to address this comment by pointing out that Islam does not believe in the national organization of non-Islamic peoples or any countries that do not follow Islamic law.

In Islamic law there are only two types of nations—a nation that is of the house of Islam or a nation that is of the house of war. We all know that America and most of the European countries are not "the house of Islam," meaning they do not live by the Islamic law; therefore, they are the "house of war."

Any good Muslim who is living according to Allah's law and the Quran will never choose loyalty to their citizenship over loyalty to Islam. This is not personal opinion; this is 100 percent Islamic law.

A good example of this is the way that Egyptians, Algerians,

Sudanese, Saudis and many others deny their citizenship and loyalty to their countries when they became members of one of the fundamentalist movements. These movements teach their members, "Islam is your flesh and blood."

All of the fundamentalist movements in the Arabic countries prohibit their members from serving in the military or defending their countries. They believe they should not support renegade and infidel countries that do not apply Islamic law to the whole country.

Shokri Moustafa, a person you will learn much more about later in the book, took this principle to an even higher level. His movement prohibited its members from working in any government job.

Muslims who have any sense of loyalty to Islam will have a hard time justifying loyalty to their country if that country is not Islamic. The true Muslim believes that the whole world is his home and that he is commanded to submit the world to the authority of Islam. A sincere believer of Islam will not die for a patch of dirt called the homeland, but he is willing to die for Islam and Islamic holy places.

When you see Palestinians fighting and dying, understand that non-Muslims or shallow Muslim Palestinians are fighting for the land, but true Muslim Palestinians (Hamas) are passionate because they are fighting the enemies of Allah and defending an Islamic holy place, i.e., the Dome of the Rock in Jerusalem.

Muslims believe that the Dome of the Rock is the third most important holy place in Islam.[4] The prophet Muhammad told his followers that Allah miraculously transported him from the Arabian Desert to this place in Jerusalem and anointed him as imam to lead prayers for all of Allah's missionaries and prophets who came from heaven that day. After the prayer, the prophet Muhammad said he went to heaven to meet with Allah. (This is known as the Miraculous Night Journey [*Al-Asrah waal MahRag*].)

Groups of Palestinians are fighting the same enemy for different reasons. One group is fighting for some land that they can call home and establish a government—perhaps a communist government, according to George Habash's leadership. Habash has a Christian name, but he is not Christian; it's just his name. Another group wants the land so it can establish a socialist government according to the mindset of the former renovation engineer and businessman, Yasser Arafat.

The final group is the die-hard Muslim Palestinians who look at the other two groups as betrayers who abuse the name of Palestinians to gain power. This group is the Hamas movement, and their leader is Sheikh Ahmed Yassin.

TELLING TRUE FROM FALSE

At this point, I think you will be able to do a much better job of telling true from false when you see what amounts to Islamic propaganda in the media.

Human Rights
Under Islam

Freedom of Speech and Freedom of Religion/
Slaves of Allah Give Up Their Rights

DURING A RECENT visit to Washington, D.C., in the
winter of 2000, I heard that the Islamic Society at
Georgetown University was hosting a rally for
American students. The speaker at the rally was an ex-Baptist
minister from Texas who had converted from Christianity to
Islam. I had never heard of anything like this before.

I immediately started thinking, *What in the world could
happen to an American Baptist pastor that would cause him
to make a decision like that? How could a man who grew up
as a free human choose bondage? How could he serve as a
pastor for all of these years in some church in Texas and then
change to Islam? I don't understand.* All of these questions
made me anxious to go hear his speech.

I took a friend, and we went to this seminar. We sat in the
middle of the room, which was packed with about three hundred students. A little less than half of the students were
devout Muslims from overseas. The young men had long
beards, and the girls wore the *hijab*.

When I laid my eyes on this man as he entered the room, I couldn't believe what I saw. He looked as if he were from the deepest part of the Middle East. He was wearing the traditional clothing that Islamic fanatics wear in Egypt. He had the long, white robe and the long, thick beard—all of it. I could not believe this man was wearing the traditional clothes of the terrorist groups. Finally they introduced him as the ex-Christian pastor. They called him Sheikh Yusef. Immediately my heart was struck with tremendous sadness, and I wondered about his family and children. What happened to them?

I listened to this man for almost an hour while he shared a very dry message that showed his tremendous ignorance of Islam and Islamic history. You could almost see it in his face that he was completely lost. He tried hard to convince a young, eager crowd that Islam is the answer to our world's problems today. He delivered an absolutely foreign picture, far from the truth of Islam, the same picture that the Islamic group deceived him with, the same picture that the Islamic organizations use to bait Westerners. The more I heard his speech, the more I prayed to God to expose this deception somehow.

After he finished his talk, he gave an opportunity for comments and questions. Mine was the first hand up. After he gave me permission to speak, I stood up and started by complimenting him on his speech. He thought that I was a Muslim from the Middle East, so he smiled and asked me to go to the front and use the microphone. That was a big mistake on his part, but I realized that it was the hand of God. I got hold of the microphone and started asking him questions.

"How long has it been since you converted to Islam?"

He replied, "Eight years."

"Good," I said. "Have you faced any type of persecution here in the U.S. since you made this decision?"

"Not at all," he said.

"Did your church or other churches commit their members to go after you and never stop until they killed you because you betrayed Christianity?"

"None of that happened," he said.

"Are there any verses in the Bible that say Christian renegades should be killed?"

"No, there are no verses in the Bible that talk about that."

Now you could see the interest building among the students, but you could see the fear on the face of this ex-pastor. At that time I introduced myself by saying, "I am a former professor of Al-Azhar University. I taught Islamic history and literature. Eight years ago I left Islam and accepted Jesus Christ as my personal Savior and Lord of my life. Do you know what kind of results I had? I immediately lost my job at the university. I was put in prison by the secret police who tortured me almost to death. The Islamic groups in Egypt and my own family pursued me and tried to kill me.

"Now it has been eight years exactly, just like you, but the difference between you and me is that I lost everything I ever had or lived for. I lost my family, job, country and my right to live. Now I am constantly on the run. I no longer have a homeland, and the sword of Islam is on my neck all the time because the Quran and the prophet Muhammad made it this way. Many times I ask myself, Why did all this happen just because I just chose to practice my rights as a human being? I chose what I wanted to believe. Look at what a price I paid and continue to pay.

"My question for you, pastor, is, What was the price you

paid? What were the results of your decision? When you made that decision, no one tried to kill you or put you in prison. The FBI did not arrest you as if you had committed a terrible crime against your country and your people. No church sentenced you to death or sent out someone to kill you with a sword because you betrayed God, the church and your people.

"You, Sheikh Yusef, are still living in your country, secure and protected by great laws. You're free to travel from state to state to share about what you believe, but I am standing before you tonight with no home and no family. I lost my life's memories. I no longer can drink the great water of the Nile or set a foot on the soil of my country. I became a victim of the Islamic law; sooner or later I will die, and that may satisfy some people and fulfill Islam.

"In my former religion, I am a betrayer. But what about you, former pastor? Let me tell you, you were blessed to be born in a free country, in a Christian family. You grew up free to make any decision you like until you made this one, to become a Muslim. Sadly, you gave up your freedom, and for what? I hope you realize that you are no longer free, because the day you think of leaving Islam to practice Christianity and your rights to choose again, you will be killed by the sword of Islam and will not be able to escape. The sword of Islam will not allow you to practice your freedom anymore, even if you're living in the United States of America. There is not a nation that could stop any Muslim from carrying out your sentence and win heaven. Now, welcome, ex-pastor and Sheikh Yusef, to the kingdom of Al Kaka and Al Hagag."

Sheikh Yusef had no idea what to say after that. I am sure he did not even understand my reference to the "kingdom of Al Kaka and Al Hagag." I said that for the benefit of the

Muslim students in the room, for they all knew what I was talking about. Al Kaka was a very ruthless military commander during the time of the second caliph, and Al Hagag was the bloodthirsty governor of Iraq during the time of Yazid. These men were responsible for the deaths of thousands and thousands of people.

HUMAN RIGHTS

Sheikh Yusef had just learned a hard truth about Islam: When you become a slave of Allah, you give up your rights. Just as a democracy is an unacceptable form of government because it is man-made, Islam says that human rights are unnecessary because they are also a man-made idea that is not found in the Quran.

Islam does not acknowledge or respect human rights, women's rights or democracy. All these are Western ideas from infidels; therefore, Muslims do not acknowledge them. That is exactly what Sayyid Qutb, the founding father of modern jihad, said in his book *Social Justice in Islam.*[1]

There is a basic principle in the Islamic law called "*Al-Qaeda Al-Faquhia,*" which states, "Anyone who denies any of the Islamic truth is an infidel." The application of this principle means that anyone who does not comply with Islam principles completely must be killed. This can be applied to:

- Muslim renegades—those who leave the Muslim faith (no freedom of religion)

- Those expressing opinions against Islam (no freedom of speech)

FREEDOM OF SPEECH

Islam is in constant battle with writers, authors and other media figures who express their opinions openly in the free world. Many people have sacrificed their lives because they had a different opinion than that of Muslim fundamentalists.

A good example of this is Dr. Naguib Mahfouz, who won the 1988 Nobel Laureate in literature. Dr. Mahfouz is an Egyptian Muslim, yet radical Muslims tried to murder him in 1994. He was on his way home from work at a university when several men attacked him, stabbing him with knives. They left him in a puddle of blood on one of Cairo's streets. Dr. Mahfouz was eighty-three years old when this happened; however, he survived.[2]

Another victim of one of the Islamic movements was Dr. Farag Foda, an Egyptian agricultural expert. Dr. Foda was a moderate Muslim who cared about the country's political survival. He decided to fight the Islamic movement through his writing. He warned Egypt, the Arabic countries and the world about the dangers of fundamentalist Islam. He wrote:

> What kind of time in our history is this? This is the time when if someone asks a question the other party answers him with bullets. Many times I asked myself, What is this that we are going through in our Egyptian history? Are we ever going to snap out of it? Is this the time that if you have an opinion, or something to say, you had better get to know how to use a machine gun first or get your black belt in the martial arts? If they think that this will make us back off or stop, they are terribly mistaken. If they think their actions will scare us, they are wrong! If they think for a second that we will rest our pens from writing or our mouths from

voicing opinions, they are expecting the impossible. This is not about courage; it's about logic. Dying in defense of democracy and unity of our nation is better than living with this stinking thinking. Dying for what is right is better than living under their stupidity and dictatorial authority. I'd rather give up the rest of my life and lay in the grave than give in to them.[3]

Dr. Farag Foda, shot to death in 1992 by Islamic fundamentalists for writing books exposing their activity.

Dr. Foda said the fundamentalists were a cancer in the body that needed to be excised before it was too late. However, Dr. Foda paid the ultimate price for his opinion. He was shot to death in 1992 by the groups he warned against. He was killed because he was not afraid to express his opinion.

(Courtesy of Sinai Publishing, Cairo, Egypt)

Dr. Foda was a great inspiration to many Egyptian writers.

SALMAN RUSHDIE

This intolerance of free speech can even cross over into non-Muslim countries. A little over a decade ago the free world was stunned when the Ayatollah Khomeini, the new leader of Iran after its revolution, made a death threat in response to a novel published in England. The book was *The Satanic*

Verses, written by a British author of Indian descent named Salman Rushdie. In his book, Rushdie criticized Islam in a sarcastic way. Khomeini promised three million dollars to whoever killed Rushdie. In response to Khomeini's threat, the British police kept Rushdie in their protection. This author has to live in great fear of the sword of Islam for the rest of his life. Even after his public apology to Muslims and Islam, he has to live in hiding.

FREEDOM OF RELIGION

If you have read this far in the book, you don't need me to tell you that there is no freedom of religion in Islam. In fact, religious persecution is commanded in the Quran. What I can add to that understanding at this point is an example from Holland. In this case, Muslim writers condemned a foreign government for offering religious freedom to former Muslims.

The parliament of Holland passed a law that grants political asylum to persons who have left Islam and converted to other religions, such as Christianity. A vehement protest was published in *The Islamic World*, a magazine published in Mecca, Saudi Arabia. In an article titled, "The Right of Political Asylum for Muslim Renegades in Holland," the magazine complained that this decision was made by two Christian political parties in Holland who were "acting as if converting to Christianity is a reason for persecution."[4] What a strange thing to say, since Islamic law states that renegades from Islam must be put to death.

The article claimed that the Christian parties in Holland were trying to entice Muslims to leave their faith in order to secure citizenship in Holland.

This wicked decision is designed to take advantage of the situation of the Muslims that live in Holland. It is about manipulating the thousands of Muslims struggling to stay legally in Holland. They are pressuring these Muslims to change their religion so that they can get legal status.

The article continued to insult and accuse the church by saying:

This law is just legalizing the agenda of the Christians and the church which did not succeed in the past to entice the Muslims by all kind of financial and material prizes to get them to change their religion. Now they are using stronger methods [citizenship].

After attacking the government of Holland by saying, "This legislation is violating the religious freedom law of human rights agreement section 19," the article ended with, "We are not surprised to see the parliament giving legal rights to the secret, wicked agenda of Christianity in Holland."

First, I would like to say, "God bless Holland and any other country that gives opportunity and protection for people to practice what they believe." Thank God that someone was merciful to these people who were forced out of their Islamic countries and homes when they accepted the love of the Lord Jesus Christ. The world needs more countries that give Muslims the right to leave Islam or search for themselves to find the true God of creation who loves mankind.

When I read an article like this, my heart goes out to the Muslim world and the tremendous tragedy of human rights in these countries. The most dangerous thing a Muslim can do is leave Islam—no matter what the reason. I personally feel for people who take the courageous step away from

Islam. These people live the rest of their lives with the sword of Islam on their necks. It is a tragedy what many have to go through for their freedom. However, God is faithful to protect them from evil.

QADDAFI GETS IN TROUBLE WITH ISLAMIC LAW

Even dictators must live within the confines of Islamic law. For example, Libya's leader Muammar Qaddafi once declared that he no longer believed in anything besides the Quran and that he had abandoned all of the prophet Muhammad's teachings (hadith).

The Islamic world was shocked. Islamic scholars at Al-Azhar University in Egypt and other Islamic authorities in Saudi Arabia were disturbed greatly. The world of Islam formed a committee of scholars to go and meet with Libya's leader so they could discuss the matter with him personally.

Sheikh Mohammed Al-Gazoly, a scholar from Al-Azhar University, led the committee to Libya. The committee warned the Libyan leader about the result of his decision. They told him that if he did not repent and take back his statement, he would fall under the law of renegades and infidels. They said that according to *Al-Qaeda Al-Faquhia* he was denying many of the Islamic truths, which would force true Muslims to kill him. In light of this information, the leader of Libya repented and took back his statement. The committee went back from Libya to Cairo and announced Qaddafi's decision to repent to the whole Islamic world.

Even a man of power like Muammar Qaddafi was not free to believe as he wished. No one can escape the terroristic law of Islam. Therefore, no Islamic nation, government or parliament will ever be able to protect a renegade Muslim from the sword of Islam. No one can stop the sword of Islam from taking the lives of ex-Muslims unless free countries follow the example of Holland and offer some protection to those people.

The amazing part is that *The Islamic World* claimed that Holland was the one violating human rights! Actually, Holland *gives* Muslims the right to practice their beliefs, but also allows them the freedom to leave Islam if they choose—a luxury they would not have in their own countries. The true fact is that Islamic nations, like Saudi Arabia (where this magazine comes from), are in absolute violation of human rights because they will never allow Christianity to be practiced in their countries. They'll never allow a church to be built in their countries, and if a Muslim even thought about changing his religion, he would be killed—make no mistake about it.

So, what is bothering the writers of this magazine? I believe the only threat this law presents to Islam is proof to the world of the tremendous persecution faced by Muslims who convert to Christianity or any other religion. As a free world that believes in human rights we should provide a safe shelter for these persecuted people.

The following is a recent list of ex-Muslims who have chosen Christianity and suffered a great deal of persecution from their countries and families.

- Egyptian professor Nahad Mohammed Ali, who wrote *My Encounter With Christ*

- Former Egyptian professor at Al-Azhar University, who wrote *Against the Tide*

- Sultan Mohammed (Paul), who wrote *Why I Became Christian*

- Ibrahim Shmrok, whose book is titled *In Search for the Truth*

- Blkis Al-Sheik, a Pakistani lady whose book is titled
  When I Got the Courage to Call God My Father

- Masood, who wrote *Captive in Christ*

There are many other stories of those who have chosen to
break the bondage of the Islamic law in their lives.

Finally, I wish I could tell *The Islamic World* magazine: Do
not let your wicked, corrupted way make you think that
everyone else is just like you. The church in Holland does not
have an agenda to force Muslims into Christianity because of
one simple fact: No one can force a Muslim to change what
is in his heart. Just because Muslims force others to change
their beliefs, not everyone else does. Just because Holland
and the West treat Muslims with respect and give them privi-
leges doesn't mean that they are trying to entice them to
change religions. I know that this is foreign thinking to you,
but it is the truth. They actually treat people well just because
they are humans.

SUMMARY

Now you have a good understanding of the core beliefs of
Islam and how the characterization of Islam in the media is
false. In the next section I want to make you an informed
person regarding the life of Muhammad. I want you to know
how this man lived and the example that he set for Muslims
to follow.

SECTION III
FOLLOWING MUHAMMAD'S EXAMPLE

Chapter 8

Arabian Culture

Taking Advantage of a Violent Mind-set

WHEN YOU ARE studying a historical figure, it is important to understand the setting and culture in which he lived. For example, Jesus lived in a Jewish community that was under the control of the Romans. His actions and teachings were influenced by the circumstances of His day; for example, He had a teaching regarding paying taxes to Rome: "Give to Caesar what is Caesar's and to God what is God's" (Mark 12:17).

So, to understand Muhammad and Islam, we need to look at the culture of the place where Islam was born. We will discover the roots of terrorism all the way back in seventh-century Arabia. (Arabia is considered to be the peninsula where the modern-day countries of Yemen, Oman, United Arab Emirates, Saudi Arabia, Kuwait and Jordan are located.) The characteristics of the tribes during this pre-Islam period of history can be described in three major categories.

The Tribal Mentality

Before Islam, southwest Asia, also known as the Arabian Desert, was not developed to the point of having any distinct nations or countries. The people were not under the authority of any type of law or government. The only authority was the tribe leader over his members. These tribes were well known for their loyalty to their own tribe cultures. In modern Islamic history, what outsiders consider to be unusual loyalty is actually deeply rooted in the Arabic culture before Islam.

Extremist

One of the stronger characteristics of Arabs in Muhammad's time was that they were known for being extremist in everything—extreme love, extreme hate and no tolerance of others who were different from them. They were not likely to accept any diversity or anyone else's beliefs. Their way was the only way.

During this time of history and culture, many Arabs excelled at poetry. One of the older poets described this characteristic of extremism and said, "We are people of no medium, and tolerance is not our way. We get our way, or we will die that day trying." They took a great pride in being extreme and wrote poems about it.

This extremist mentality did not change at all after Islam. As a matter of fact, Islam embraced many of the core characteristics of this Arabic culture. There was no moderation, no reconciliation with others. If two people had a fight, no one would ever walk away. They didn't have the mentality to sit and discuss and sort out a problem. Their attitude was, "Give me my way, or give me death!" As a result, Islamic history is full of bloodshed.

Many non-Arab Muslims, such as Iranians, Afghans, Pakistani, Indians and others, have adapted to and adopted these behaviors as the way of their new religion.

CONSTANT POWER STRUGGLE AND FIGHTING

Being courageous and violent was a sign of manhood in seventh-century Arabia. The people of this culture considered being quick to fight as a necessity for survival. Only the strongest survived; therefore, these tribes fought constantly as a way of existence. This mentality was manifested into a basic lifestyle.

- Defend your own tribe and its territory.

- Plunder the possessions of those you defeat. Many individuals and groups would invade others to gain position and wealth.

Islam did not change any of these characteristics or influence the behavior of the Arabs. Instead, Islam embraced the Arab mentality and used it to accomplish its agenda. Jihad (fighting the enemy of Allah to death) as a core belief of Islam came to the Arabic mentality not as a new behavior but as one with which they were very familiar. Islam called on the Arabs to act out their courage and violent ways.

The majority of the Arabs entered Islam so that they would be rewarded with the possessions of people who would not submit to Islam. Islamic history tells us that many times during the early days of Islam, the proper way to divide spoils was an area of controversy among the Arab Muslims.

So we see that Muhammad was born into a culture where conquest and bloodshed were the norm. Now let's see how those norms were incorporated into Islam through the concept of jihad.

Muhammad Declares Jihad

Jihad Fully Developed in Muhammad's Lifetime

THE IMMIGRATION OF Muhammad from Mecca to Medina was a defining moment in the history of Islam. Everything in the mind-set of the prophet of Islam changed—especially his attitude toward the unbelieving people around him.

In Mecca, Muhammad never spoke of jihad. There was no talk of holy war because he did not have military strength, and his movement was small and weak in society. But in Medina, where he built an army, the major topic of Quranic revelation was jihad and fighting the enemy. Revelations increasingly served to motivate Muslims to fight.

Let's compare the differences between Muhammad's life in Mecca and his life in Medina.

- **Mecca:** He invited people to be a part of Islam by preaching.
  Medina: He persuaded people to convert by the sword.

- **Mecca**: He acted like a priest, living a life of prayer, fasting and worship.
  Medina: He behaved like a military commander, personally leading twenty-seven attacks.

- **Mecca**: He had only one wife, Khadija, for those twelve years.
  Medina: He married twelve more women in ten years.

- **Mecca**: He fought against idol worship.
  Medina: He fought against People of the Book (Jews and Christians).

Muhammad's move from Mecca to Medina changed Islam into a political movement. Dr. Omar Farouk wrote in his book *The Arabs and Islam:*

> The immigration of the prophet of Islam from Mecca to Medina is of great importance in Islamic history. It marks a great revolution in the nature of Islam. Islam went from a religious and spiritual revelation to a political agenda.

I am now going to give you the history of jihad as it was developed and defined in Muhammad's life. Remember, for about twenty-two years Muhammad received Quranic verses from the angel Gabriel. The philosophy of jihad was developed progressively, just as Muhammad's political position was developed progressively. As Muhammad's position in society grew stronger, the revelations about jihad became broader and grander.

MUHAMMAD'S PROBLEMS IN MECCA

One must ask, "Why did Muhammad leave Mecca?" Muhammad spent ten to twelve years in Mecca, persuading people to follow Islam without killing them or demanding any taxes from them. His message was one of repentance, patience and forgiveness. However, there was great tension between him and the tribe he came from. This was the biggest tribe of the area–Quraysh. Many people were abandoning idol worship and following Islam, which the tribal leaders did not like.

At first they tried to make a deal with Muhammad. "We'll make you a king," the tribal leaders told him, "but don't talk about Islam anymore. Or if you want to be wealthy, we'll give you money and make you the wealthiest man in Arabia."

Muhammad happened to be standing next to his uncle when they said this, and he replied, "Oh, my uncle, if they bring the sun and put it in my right hand and bring the moon and put it in my left hand, I will not give up my revelation."

Muhammad negotiated with the leaders from A.D. 620 to 622, but they never reached an agreement.[1]

The tribe of Quraysh began to persecute him. They threw dirt on his head while he was praying, and they spit on him. They tried to kill him several times. One time they had a lady invite him for a meal and put poison in the lamb she served him. The Quran makes reference to Muhammad's problems at this time:

> And (remember) when the disbelievers plotted against you (O Muhammad) to imprison you, or to kill you, or to get you out (from your home, i.e., Makkah); they were plotting and Allah too was plotting; and Allah is the Best of those who plot.
>
> —SURAH 8:30, *THE NOBLE QURAN*

Muhammad did not leave Mecca without thinking, however. He had a plan for what he would do after he left.

FIRST REVELATION OF JIHAD:
REPAY THOSE WHO MISTREAT YOU

Muhammad spent his first year in Medina building up his military strength. The goal of his first jihad, or holy war, was to take revenge on Quraysh, the tribe that had persecuted him. This attitude is no surprise because Muhammad was still influenced by the Arab mentality I described earlier. ("If you cause me one trouble, I will cause you two troubles.")

The Quraysh tribe created wealth through trade. Each year they took one trip to Yemen and one trip to Syria. They took a large caravan of things to sell at their destination, and brought home another load of things to sell at home. They carried a lot of money and valuables.

Muhammad planned to ambush one of the caravans returning to Mecca. He and his army laid wait for them in the Valley of Badr. However, the caravan leader heard about the trap and successfully went home by a different road.

The tribal leaders were very happy the caravan got home, but they were very angry with Muhammad. They decided to teach him a lesson to let everyone in Arabia see that no one played games with the Quraysh tribe. Mecca sent their army to fight Muhammad at Badr. To their shock, Muhammad won a great victory and killed most of the enemy army.

Everyone in Arabia heard about the battle—and they recognized that Muhammad was now the most powerful man in Arabia because he had defeated the most powerful tribe.

THE SECOND REVELATION OF JIHAD:
CONQUER YOUR REGION

After this victory, Muhammad said the angel Gabriel brought him a new message: that he must fight every tribe in Arabia and make them all submit to Islam. Muhammad declared, "There will not be two religions in Arabia. Arabia will submit only to Islam."[2] As a result, Muhammad no longer focused mainly on converting heathen or idol worshipers. Now the Jews and Christians became targets of persuasion.

This development of jihad came through the following Quranic verse:

> Fight against those who (1) believe not in Allah, (2) nor in the Last Day, (3) nor forbid that which has been forbidden by Allah and His Messenger (Muhammad) (4) and those who acknowledge not the religion of truth (i.e. Islam) among the people of the Scripture (Jews and Christians), until they pay the *Jizyah* [tax] with willing submission, and feel themselves subdued.
> —SURAH 9:29, *THE NOBLE QURAN*

At first glance, this verse is a little hard to understand in English, but it will be very clear after I explain it. This verse says Muslims must fight four kinds of people:

1. Those who don't believe in Allah

2. Those who don't believe in the last day

3. Those who do things that Allah and Muhammad have forbidden

4. Those who don't acknowledge Islam as the truth, i.e., "people of the Scripture," who are the Jews and Christians

Muhammad gave people three options:

1. They could accept the message of Islam.

2. They could remain Jews or Christians but pay a special tax (*jizyah*), which is traditionally levied once a year.

3. They could die. (The phrase "and feel themselves subdued" is much stronger in Arabic than in this English translation. The Arabic word means something like "abject subjection." It carries the idea of someone cowering in fear before a greater power. If abject subjection is not achieved, then death follows.)

The results of Muhammad's options were that the majority accepted the message of Islam, the wealthy unbelievers paid high taxes, and the rest were forced to go to war.

TAXING CHRISTIANS TODAY

The tax against Christians is not something that was just practiced in ancient times. Fanatic groups in Egypt still go to Christians and ask for the tax. They will meet with the Christian and explain, "You are Christian. We are Muslim. This is a Muslim country. Our job is to practice the law of Islam. The law says you have two choices—convert to Islam or remain in your faith. It's OK with us if you choose to remain in your faith, but you must pay tax every year to the Islamic authority."

The Egyptian government isn't trying to collect the tax, but these independent groups have taken it upon themselves because the government isn't doing it.

So the Christian is presented with the tax, which is usually a sizeable sum of money based on his income. The Christian may say, "I don't have the money right now. Give me a few days to pull it together." So the radicals will go away and come back in a few days.

The Christian may again say, "Please, give me another week." So they will go away and come back in a week. But if the Christian still doesn't have the money, there are no more chances. You can be sure they will come back and kill him—probably shoot him to death.

I have a Christian friend from Egypt who is now a university professor in the United States. His two Christian brothers, a medical doctor and a pharmacist, were living in Egypt, and the radicals came and asked for the tax. These Christians refused, and they were both killed. This was just two or three years ago.

FINANCING JIHAD

The tax on unbelievers was one way Muhammad raised money. But his most important source of income was plundering after battle. This was his economic lifeblood, just as oil is the economic life of the Gulf countries today. They did not farm, work trades or conduct business. They fought.

Part of their profit came from slave trading. When invading an enemy country, they killed all males and took the women and children as slaves. During that time the Arabian Desert became famous for slave trading.

Of his plundering, Muhammad said:

> All income that comes by the hooves of horses and the point of the sword is a gift from Allah. Allah provides for those who fight. But if they go back to their old trades, they will just earn a living the normal way.[3]

Muhammad had an agreement with his military regarding

the plunder taken from defeated enemies. Muhammad got to keep 20 percent, and the army could divide the remaining 80 percent among themselves. This sounds pretty good, except his army could have as many as ten thousand men. So each man in the army got .008 percent compared to Muhammad's 20 percent.

Muhammad's army started rebelling and complaining against him because they said they didn't get to keep enough of the plunder. The situation looked as if it would get out of control until Muhammad received a new revelation.

> And know that out of all the booty that you may acquire (in war), a fifth share is assigned to Allah,—and to the Messenger, and to near relatives, orphans, the needy, and the wayfarer…
>
> —SURAH 8:41, ALI TRANSLATION

This entire surah (chapter) was titled "The Spoils of War." It specifically mentions the Battle of Badr. If you want a good overview of the military mind-set of Muhammad, read this chapter.

The invasion of Uhud

This was the second war that the prophet Muhammad and new converts fought against the Arabs who rejected the call of Islam. After the fight the military leaders and the personal guard of Muhammad faced a major conflict. The disagreement was over plundering the possessions of the enemy. The military leaders told the personal guard of Muhammad that they should take part in the plundering of possessions. "If we didn't fight, there would be no victory," they argued. Muhammad had to solve the problem by ordering the military leaders and his personal guard to split the plunder equally after this battle.[4]

The invasion of Honeen

Historian Ibn Hisham wrote in particular about the invasion of Honeen. The Muslim military lost due to their hastiness to plunder the possessions of the enemy before the battle was finalized. When the Muslims went after the possessions, the enemy ambushed them and defeated them. Prophet Muhammad motivated his military by telling them, "Whoever kills someone is entitled to plunder his possessions."[5]

Hiring help for battle

Dr. Solomon Basheer mentions that Muhammad even hired other tribes to help him fight, motivating them with a share of the plunder:

> Sometimes the Arabic tribes agreed to get involved with Muhammad and support him in the battles. These tribes made contracts with the Muslim leaders regarding what percentage of the plunder they could take.[6]

This method of fund-raising continued after Muhammad's death. The second leader of Islam (Umar ibn al-Khattab) is credited with many conquests for Islam. This leader also made agreements with other tribes to fight for Islam.

> Jarir Bin Abdullah came and asked the second Muslim leader after the death of Muhammad (Umar ibn al-Khattab), "If I go to Iraq with my people to fight for Islam, can we keep 25 percent of the plunder?" Umar agreed.[8]

Umar promised Muslims that they would profit from the people they conquered.

Allah brought Muslims to the world to conquer and rule and populate the world. If any nation opposes the will of Allah and refuses to be Muslim, they will be the slaves of Muslims and pay tax to the Islamic authority. These nations are going to work hard, and you will benefit.[7]

THE FINAL REVELATION OF JIHAD: CONQUER THE WORLD

The last step in the development of jihad was when jihad stopped being regional and went worldwide. This change was based on a new Quranic verse received by Muhammad:

> Fight them until there is no more *Fitnah* (disbelief and polytheism, i.e. worshipping others besides Allah) and the religion (worship) will be for Allah Alone [in the whole of the world].
>
> —SURAH 8:39, *THE NOBLE QURAN*

As a result, Muhammad told his followers:

> I command by Allah to go and fight all the people of the world until they confess there is no God but Allah, and I am his messenger, and to pray five times a day and to give alms. And if they do that, their blood will be spared from me.[9]

The Muslims put these revelations into practice right away. They took jihad outside of Arabia, attacking many countries in Asia, Africa and Europe. This was the whole world at the time.

In all, Muhammad personally led twenty-seven battles. In addition, he sent out his army forty-seven times without him (that's about seven times a year).[10] Muhammad's reign ended in A.D. 632 with his death. Despite his military activity, he did not have a battle-related death. History records that he actually succumbed to an extended fever.

SUMMARY

After reviewing the culture and some of the characteristics of the Arabic people prior to Muhammad, we have a deeper understanding of the bloody history of Islam. Disagreements and misunderstandings often led to terrorist acts among the pre-Islam Arabic people due to their predisposition to act emotionally and violently as a whole.

Because Islam entitled them to the defeated enemies' possessions, the constant struggle for power among Arab tribes grew stronger and more brutal. Not only did they attack non-Muslims, but the early Muslim tribes also attacked each other. An example of this was the constant battle between the Ammoweyeen and the Hashmeyeen, both of the tribe of Quraysh.

This culture readily accepted the philosophy of jihad that was revealed to Muhammad. These were progressive revelations of Quranic verses over a period of about twenty-two years. The progressive steps were:

1. Fight those who persecuted you (in Medina).

2. Conquer those who reject Islam in your region (the Arabian Desert).

3. Conquer the world in the name of Islam.

No Quranic revelation contradicted this final command of jihad, so it is still the goal of Islam today.

The Ultimate Goal of Islam

Worldwide Submission to Islam

JUST AS IN the days of Muhammad, the fundamentalist followers of Islam today are pursuing world conquest. The best way I can describe this mind-set is to let one of the leaders say it in his words.

One of the clearest writers and thinkers of modern jihad is Mawlana Abul Ala Mawdudi, the founder of Pakistan's fundamentalist movement. He has written many books and is one of Islam's most well-known scholars. The entire Islamic world considers him a leader who will be remembered throughout history. These are his words:[1]

> Islam is not a normal religion like the other religions in the world, and Muslim nations are not like normal nations. Muslim nations are very special because they have a command from Allah to rule the entire world and to be over every nation in the world.

He points out that the purpose of the revolution is not to set up a particular person in power or to decide which countries will be better off than other countries.

> Islam is a revolutionary faith that comes to destroy any government made by man. Islam doesn't look for a nation to be in better condition than another nation. Islam doesn't care about the land or who owns the land. The goal of Islam is to rule the entire world and submit all of mankind to the faith of Islam. Any nation or power in this world that tries to get in the way of that goal, Islam will fight and destroy.
>
> In order for Islam to fulfill that goal, Islam can use every power available every way it can be used to bring worldwide revolution. This is jihad.

Mawdudi also expressed the idea that Islam is a political system and way of life that must replace all other ways of life.

> Islam is not just a spiritual religion; Islam is a way of life. It is a heavenly system revealed to our world through the angel Gabriel, and the responsibility of Muslims is to destroy any other system in the world and to replace it with the Islamic system.
>
> Everyone who believes in Islam in this manner can be a member of *Jamaat-i-Islami* [the Pakistani fundamentalist movement founded by the author]. I don't want anybody to think that Muslims who join the party of God are just normal Muslim missionaries or normal preachers in the mosque or people who write articles. The party of God is a group established by Allah himself to take the truth of Islam in one hand and to take the sword in the other hand and destroy the kingdoms of evil and the kingdoms of mankind and to replace them with the Islamic system. This group is going to destroy the false gods and make Allah the only God.

By saying "false gods," the author is referring to political leaders who are not under Islamic authority, such as presidents or prime ministers of Western countries.

As you can see, Islam is the faith of struggle, revolution and war. Islam doesn't want a little piece of the world—it wants it all.

CHRISTIANS AS TARGETS

Christians are a target in the goal of world conquest because they resist conversion. This perspective is not just implied. It is explicitly stated.

In 1980 there was a meeting of the Muslim International World Society in Lehore, Pakistan. *Le Vigaro,* a prominent French newspaper, reported that the conference discussed ways that the Islamic world could end the existence of the Christian minority in the Muslim world or force them to become Muslim. Their timetable for achieving this was the end of the second millennium.

The chairman of this society sued the French newspaper in 1984, claiming that the report was false. But I believe the newspaper reported the truth, because that is truly the agenda of Islam.

Another example of the mind-set of converting Christians to Islam occurred during the Lebanese Civil War. This war between Christians and Muslims lasted twenty years, and no one could figure out how to get them to stop—not the United Nations or even the other Arab countries.

The leader of Libya, Muammar Qaddafi, considers himself to be a great thinker, and he announced one day that he had a solution to the problem. His solution was for the Christians to convert to Islam and then they would be brothers and sisters with the Muslims and the fighting would stop. Qaddafi said:

> I hope there is a new generation of Lebanese Christians
> who will wake up one day and realize Arabs cannot be
> Christians and Christians cannot be Arabs, so then they
> will convert to Islam and be true Arabs.[2]

METHODS OF JIHAD

We've seen that jihad was established in the Quran and that
it involves world domination. Jihad is now the call for every
Muslim. Now let us see how jihad is practiced in three stages
in modern times.

The Three Stages
of Jihad

How a Weakened Muslim Minority
Takes Over

I F YOU LOOK at Muslim countries around the world, you will see that they are in one of the following three stages of jihad. (My source for these stages is Islamic theology based on the Quran.)

WEAKENED STAGE

This stage applies to Muslims when they are a weak, small minority living in a non-Islamic society. In this case overt jihad is not the call of the hour. Muslims submit to the law of the land, but they work to increase their numbers.

At this stage, Muslims follow the word given to Muhammad in Mecca: "There is no compulsion in religion" (Surah 2:256, *The Noble Quran*). You have probably heard people in the media quoting this verse to prove that Islam does not compel, or force, anyone to convert.

Another key verse Muhammad received at this time was Surah 5:105:

> O you who believe! Take care of your ownselves. If you
> follow the (right) guidance [and enjoin what is right
> (Islamic Monotheism and all that Islam orders one to
> do) and forbid what is wrong (polytheism, disbelief
> and all that Islam has forbidden)] no hurt can come to
> you from those who are in error. The return of you all is
> to Allah, then He will inform you about (all) that which
> you used to do.
>
> —*The Noble Quran*

This verse was a response to Muslims in Mecca who were
wondering what to do about all the unbelievers around
them. It basically told them, "Be responsible for yourself.
Don't worry about the infidels around you. You and they will
all go before Allah one day and be judged by your works."

These verses speak of living quietly and at peace with
unbelievers; however, we need to remember that
Muhammad received these words when Muslims were a
small, weak group in Mecca. After his movement gained
strength, Muhammad received new words that canceled out
(*nasikh*) these verses.

PREPARATION STAGE

This stage is when the Muslims are a reasonably influential
minority. Because their future goal is direct confrontation
with the enemy, they make preparations in every possible
area—financial, physical, military, mental and any other area.

> Let not the Unbelievers think that they can get the
> better (of the godly): they will never frustrate (them).
> *Against them make ready your strength to the utmost
> of your power*, including steeds of war, to strike terror
> into (the hearts of) the enemies, of Allah and your ene-

mies, and others besides whom you may not know, but whom Allah knows.

—SURAH 8:59–60, ALI TRANSLATION, EMPHASIS ADDED

The Noble Quran includes some interesting commentary. Notice the words in parentheses:

And make ready against them all you can of power, including steeds of war *(tanks, planes, missiles, artillery)* to threaten the enemy of Allah…

—SURAH 8:60, EMPHASIS ADDED

This commentary should confirm for the reader that Muslims are practicing this verse in modern times.

JIHAD STAGE

This stage is when Muslims are a minority with strength, influence and power. At this stage every Muslim's duty is to actively fight the enemy, overturning the system of the non-Muslim country and establishing Islamic authority.

This stage is based on the final revelation that Allah received concerning jihad, which is Surah 9:5. Though I quoted this verse earlier, it is so significant in Islamic thinking that it bears repeating:

Fight and slay the Pagans wherever you find them, and seize them, beleaguer them, and lie in wait for them in every stratagem (of war)…

—ALI TRANSLATION

Muslims are commanded to kill anyone who chooses not to convert to Islam. The verse says "wherever you find them." There are no geographical limits.

MUHAMMAD'S EXAMPLE

These three stages are exactly what the prophet Muhammad lived out. At first he showed no animosity to his enemies (Phase 1). After he left Mecca he spent his first year in Medina preparing his army (Phase 2). Then he declared jihad, went back to fight his enemies, completely conquered Mecca and brought it under his authority (Phase 3).

LEBANON

The recent history of the modern nation of Lebanon can provide us a good example of the three stages in practice.

Stage 1: Muslims cooperate with the Christian majority.

If you had visited Lebanon before their civil war you would have seen the Hawaii of the Middle East. The capital, Beirut, was called the Paris of the Middle East. Lebanon was the most beautiful natural setting around.

The Muslim minority lived in harmony with the Christian majority. That was because the Muslims were a weak minority with no power. There were no talks about jihad, or holy war, those days in Lebanon.

Stage 2: Muslims get outside help to prepare for attack.

Slowly but surely, in the 1970s the Islamic minority started the preparation stage by getting support from Libya on one side and Iran on the other. Not too long after that the Lebanese civil war began.

Stage 3: Muslims wage war against unbelievers.

The world watched as the beautiful country of Lebanon was divided into many pieces. Muslims denied any loyalty to their Christian brothers and sisters. They started militant groups that were after one goal—overturning the government and establishing an Islamic country.

One Islamic group was called Amal and was led by Nabih Bary; there was another Shiite group called Hizbollah, which was led by Sheikh Hassan Nasrallah.

Twenty years of war followed, but Muslims did not succeed in their mission.

Compromise (Back to Stage 1)

Right now Lebanon has a secular government with a Christian president and a Muslim prime minister. There is peace for the moment because they established a government that included all the warring parties.

They even made the founder of Amal the president of the parliament. They allow Hizbollah to exist in South Lebanon because, they say, "We must have them there to defend against Israel."

JUSTIFYING DECEIT

The three stages of jihad show how circumstances are used to determine correct behavior. Another example of this in the Islamic mind-set is the use of deceit. Islam justifies lying under certain circumstances. In the next chapter you will learn what those circumstances are and how they apply to jihad.

Chapter 12

When Lies Are Justified

Deceit As a Part of War and to Avoid Trouble

MUSLIMS BELIEVE THAT war means deception, so lying is an important element of war in Islam. In this chapter we will look at the particular circumstances in which Muslims are permitted to lie.

LYING TO NON-MUSLIMS WHILE LIVING IN A NON-MUSLIM COUNTRY

Philosopher Ibn Taymiyah (1263–1328) wrote a book titled *The Sword on the Neck of the Accuser of Muhammad*. In it he described how Muslims should live in the weakened stage.

> Believers when in a weakened stage in a non-Muslim country should forgive and be patient with people of the book [i.e., Jews and Christians] when they insult Allah and his prophet by any means. Believers should lie to people of the book to protect their lives and religion.[1]

In other words, it's OK to lie to non-Muslims to protect yourself when you are a minority in their country.

There's a simple Islamic proverb that says, "If you can't cut your enemies' hand, kiss it."[2] This is clear in the prophet Muhammad's life and his teaching in Mecca and after. The peaceful lamb of Mecca, after immigrating to Medina, became a roaring lion that threatened the whole Arabian Desert.

I never experienced living in the weakened state because Muslims are a strong majority in Egypt where I grew up. We Muslims practiced our beliefs in any way that we liked. The Christians were the weakened minority. I never had a reason to lie to Christians, but I witnessed every day how these Christians lived under strong persecution as a minority in an Islamic country.

On the other hand, those practicing Islam in the United States, Canada, Europe, Australia and South Africa are in the weakened stage. These Muslims are very good at presenting themselves as loving, caring and forgiving people. They compromise any conflict between the image they want to present and what they truly believe.

They get along with Christians and Jews as if they were brothers. They present Islam to these countries as the answer to all humanity's problems. These Westernized Muslims present their religion as if it stands for mercy, freedom, fairness and reconciliation. They portray Islam as a religion that does not show prejudice to any race or culture.

LYING ABOUT PEACE AGREEMENTS

Muslim groups will use peace talks or peace agreements to buy time so they can make new plans, prepare and position themselves for victory. Muslim military leaders will tell the other side whatever it wants to hear in order to buy time, but when it comes time to deliver what is agreed on, you will see a different story.

Our modern history has witnessed many of these peace agreements that resulted in nothing happening. An example that comes to my mind is all of the agreements that took place between the Muslim groups in South Lebanon, the Hizbollah and Amal organizations. Another great example is the nine years of peace talks between Iraq and Iran, which resulted only in a vicious war.

I clearly remember what happened in Egypt during the fight between the government and the Islamic Group (*al-Gama'a al Islamiyya*). The leaders of the Islamic Group announced that they had suspended hostilities and were willing to meet at the negotiating table. That was nothing but buying time to regroup and go after the government even more than before. The Islamic Group used lies and tricks based on their understanding of the Quran and the prophet Muhammad's life teaching and history.

Many people may disagree with how I am portraying Islam; however, these facts are very clear in Islamic law. Let's see how Muhammad used lying, since his actions are part of the basis of Islamic law.

DENYING ISLAMIC FAITH

The first time that the prophet Muhammad permitted denying Islam or him as a prophet was with Amar Ben Yasser.[3] Yasser, who was one of Muhammad's friends, was captured and held hostage by the tribe of Quraysh. The tribe tortured Yasser, so he denied Muhammad and Islam to gain freedom.

As soon as they set him free, he went back to Muhammad and confessed what had happened. Prophet Muhammad told Yasser that if that ever happened to him again he should do exactly what he did with no shame.

At a different time, the prophet Muhammad heard that one of his enemies (Shabban Bin Kalad Al-Handi) was preparing his troops to fight the Muslims. Muhammad sent Abed Allah Bin Anis Algahni to assassinate this enemy. Algahni asked the prophet Muhammad to describe the man that he was supposed to kill. Muhammad told him to go and join the enemies' troops, curse Islam and Muhammad, and that he would find Al-Handi that way.

Prophet Muhammad's messenger went to the enemies' camp. When he identified the leader, he struck up a conversation and cursed Muhammad and his people. To make a long story short, Alghani was able to build a close enough relationship with his victim to cut off his head when he was sleeping. He brought the head to the prophet.

We see here that the prophet Muhammad's messenger used lying—denying the faith and cursing prophet Muhammad—in order to accomplish his mission.[4]

MUSLIMS DECEIVING OTHER MUSLIMS

When it comes to war, Muslims will lie to other Muslims if necessary. This explains an incident between President Saddam Hussein of Iraq and President Hosni Mubarak of Egypt. Mubarek visited Hussein in Baghdad on the day before Iraq invaded Kuwait. Hussein promised Mubarak that he would not invade Kuwait, yet no sooner had Mubarak arrived home in Cairo than he heard that the invasion took place.

Hussein lied to his fellow Muslim, and he didn't even keep his word for twenty-four hours. That made the Egyptian president truly angry.[5]

GENERAL BELIEF ABOUT LYING

As you can see, Islam justifies and practices lying under war circumstances. The general attitude about lying can be illustrated by a story about one of Muhammad's favorite wives, Aiysha.

Lying is good if it is going to keep evil away.

Imam Gazoli Saibin states:

> Know this that lying is not sin by itself, but if it brings harm to you it could be ugly. However, you can lie if that will keep you from evil or if it will result in prosperity.[7]

We know from Islamic history and the prophet Muhammad's autobiography that major jealousy took place between two of Muhammad's wives, Aiysha and Zeneb. Zeneb's sister started a rumor that Aiysha had an affair with another man.[6] Her motive was to help out her sister because the punishment for adultery in Islam is stoning (Surah 24:2).

Aiysha denied having the affair, even though people close to the situation, including Muhammad's best friend, were sure she had done it. Lying was acceptable because it would keep the evil of stoning away.

SUMMARY

As you can see, lying and deceit are a part of the Islamic mind-set. This fact can be difficult for the Western mind to accept. Another difficult concept for the Western mind is the fact that a mosque is not just for religious activity. Mosques are used to support jihad, which was even made evident during the U.S. bombing of Afghanistan.

Chapter 13

Muhammad's Use of Mosques

House of Worship/House of War

During the U.S. bombing campaign in Afghanistan, the U.S. military bombed a mosque on October 23, 2001. The Lebanese News Center complained, "People who were praying inside were killed and injured."[1] On the other hand, the *Washington Post* said that, according to recent refugees, the Taliban had begun moving military equipment and personnel to mosques, schools and other civilian sites to avoid attack.[2]

This incident illustrates two things: the use of deceit during war and the use of a mosque for war efforts.

A MOSQUE ISN'T A CHURCH

Most of the Muslims who are interviewed by Western media present Islam as a religion only. They emphasize the heart as the center of the Islamic teaching and the mosque as the worship place of the Muslims, just like a church or a synagogue.

However, the mosque during the prophet Muhammad's time was not just the place of worship. It was also a place to store weapons and make military plans. When Muhammad was in Medina, he used the mosque as headquarters for all of his wars. Even after his death, his successors used the mosques for the same purposes.

A mosque in Islam is the center for worship, justice, war strategy and government. This is because Islam is both a religion and government. Islam is a pen and a sword.

Prophet Muhammad made it clear to Muslims that the mosque isn't like a synagogue or a church. At his mosque in Medina (the second holiest site in Islam today), he planned his war strategy, held court and received visiting tribal leaders. It was like the Pentagon, the White House and the Supreme Court all in one place. The Islamic world was ruled from the mosque.

When there was an order to fight, the announcement was made at the mosque. The rulers after Muhammad continued this practice. Throughout Islamic history you can see that all movements of jihad came out of the mosque.

EGYPTIAN MILITANTS' USE OF MOSQUES

In modern times, mosques are still used as centers of war. The Egyptian Islamic groups are a good example. In 1986 the Egyptian police received orders from Zaki Bedr, prime minister of national security, to attack different mosques in southern Egypt because militant Islamic groups were using them.

The attack against the mosques caused much anger among moderate Muslims. The following dialogue occurred in the Egyptian Parliament between Bedr, who ordered the strikes, and the opposing party representative, Mohammed Mahfoz Helmy. Helmy explained why he was questioning Bedr's actions:

The motive of my questions is not to accuse you of doing wrong, but as a representative of the people, we demand an explanation of the action of the administration of security in southern Egypt. The way that your administration surprised Muslim worshipers inside of the mosque and arrested them was an insult to Islam.

Bedr answered by saying:

We had accurate information that these radical Islamic groups used the mosque to plan and operate an attack on the citizens and the police. To be more specific, on Friday, October 31, 1986, we monitored the members of these groups taking weapons and people to the mosque to prepare for a major attack on the citizens of Assout and the police force. As a result of these attacks, six high-ranking officers and seventeen solders were wounded. However, we confiscated from the mosque many illegal handguns, and we found dead bodies of the citizens. We arrested fifty-seven members of these groups. After a short investigation we released two of these fifty-seven and jailed the other fifty-five.

The prime minister of national security told the Egyptian parliament that this wasn't the only time a mosque had been used as a military base. Five days before this invasion, another invasion was conducted.

October 26, 1986, we received accurate information about a major plan for the Islamic radicals to destroy and attack the police and the citizens right after the Friday prayer. This information was enough for us to send out some of our best forces to stop these plans and keep national security under control. Moments after the arrival of the forces they discovered the gathering of 120 members of the Islamic Group inside the mosque. These members did not allow general worshipers to enter the mosque to pray that day. We monitored them carefully and stood by to see how they would act. As soon as they made their first step to come out of the mosque and carry out their plans, we immediately attacked the mosque and arrested 121 people.

The prime minister of national security addressed the parliament by saying:

What these two incidents mean to me and my administration is that mosques are the gathering place and the centers for these radical Muslims. As long as I am in position, I will not tolerate it. We should stand together and unite in opinion to fight the threat of terrorism to our country even if they are raising the banner of Islam. I do not attempt to deny my responsibility for these attacks as my opponent's party claimed, but as a citizen of this great nation of Egypt I call the opponent's party to unite with our government and stand strong in the face of these threats of terrorism to keep our nation secure.[3]

What we saw in this documented modern history was that the Islamic Group movement (al-Gama'a al Islamiyya) used the mosque as a place of planning attacks and hiding weapons—following the example of the prophet Muhammad.

SECTION IV

THE DEVELOPMENT OF MODERN JIHAD

Forefathers of
Terrorism

A.D. *600s to 1800s*

YOU ARE ABOUT to embark on a guided tour through twelve hundred years of Islamic history. Along the way you will discover the events and movements that have produced the principles of jihad that are practiced today. This chapter, which covers the time from Muhammad to the 1800s, will explain:

- The logic behind attacking leaders and governments who reject Islam, Muhammad or the Quran

- Justification for killing women and children

- The belief that you should fight even if you know you will lose

- The suicide mission by Muhammad's grandson

- Eleventh-century terrorists who got high on marijuana before going to attack their enemies

GOOD REASONS TO KILL

Let's begin our tour by taking a few snapshots from the life of Muhammad. As you visualize these scenes from Muhammad's life, you may find it interesting to imagine what it would have been like if Jesus had behaved the same way.

When Muhammad moved to Medina in A.D. 622, he found many strong Jewish clans there who resisted him. The leader of a clan called Ebniah-El-Tadyiar resisted with words. He excelled in poetry and its use in condemning Muhammad and his teachings.

This poetry got him in trouble with a powerful and competitive Jewish clan in the area (El-Aouse), which had converted to Islam. (Yes, it's true; they converted.) When they heard this poetry, they planned to murder the author (Kahbb-Ebniah-El Ashrafi) in order to win the favor of Muhammad. They persuaded the poet's own brother to kill him. (Their mother was Jewish, but their father was Arabian.)

Because the clans were so competitive for Muhammad's favor, a rival Jewish clan that had also converted to Islam (El-Khazrahg) looked for someone else Muhammad did not like in order to kill him as well. Abbah Rafah Salam was the second victim killed in order to keep Muhammad's favor.

In the meantime, the prophet Muhammad ordered another man to go and kill a lady named Ossmah (daughter of Marawan), because she also used her poetry to condemn Muhammad and his teachings.[1]

The murder of the Jewish poet was perceived negatively among Arabs. Muhammad's first cousin, Ali ibn Abi Talib, who was among the first followers of Muhammad, assumed the responsibility of defending Muhammad's orders to murder. He told the people that God sent the angel Gabriel to Muhammad and commanded this man's death. Then he wrote a poem to confirm that this murder was God's command.

These three murders established a basic principle of behavior.

> **PRINCIPLE: Anyone who conflicts with, disagrees with or does not support Muhammad and his teachings should be killed.**

MUHAMMAD PERMITS KILLING WOMEN AND CHILDREN

Let's see what the prophet of Islam said about killing women and children of the enemy.

Prophet Muhammad was once asked if it was OK to kill women and children of those who were polytheistic (believing in many gods) or infidels. He said, "I consider them as of their parents." In other words, if the parents were infidels, then it was permissible to kill their children.[2] Because the prophet of Islam believed this, this is what Osama bin Laden and Al-Qaeda believe about killing women and children.

KILLING LEADERS WHO BREAK ISLAMIC LAW

Muhammad died in A.D. 632 after a long fever, according to historical records. The third leader to succeed him, Uthman ibn Affan, experienced much protest against his leadership and governing of the people. He was accused of mishandling money, moral failures and other transgressions. A group of Muslims from many different nations surrounded his house and asked for his resignation. He swore by Allah that he would not respond to this threat and refused to give up leadership.

Within a few days they went back into the house and found him meditating and reading the Quran. They killed him there.

> **PRINCIPLE: It is right to murder a governor or leader who is not in compliance with Islamic law.**

After his death, the Islamic nation was never the same. This was the fork in the road where the Islamic faith was divided forever.

FALSE TREATY CAUSES SPLIT BETWEEN MUSLIMS

After the murder of Islam's third leader, Muhammad's first cousin, Ali ibn Abi Talib, was chosen to be the fourth leader of Islam. Ali was revered by many because he was Muhammad's closest assistant, like his right arm.

The governor of El-Sham (Syria) opposed this appointment. He was from the same family as the previous leader who was murdered (Uthman). So the governor of El-Sham asked Ali to arrest the people who killed Uthman and judge them. Ali replied, "There are thousands; whom am I going to arrest? Whom am I going to judge?"

This started war. The governor, Muawiya ibn Abi Sufyan, fought many battles with Ali.

Ali's group became divided. Part of them opposed fighting and petitioned Ali to stop the war. They wanted to debate for a solution, choosing a representative from both sides who knew the Quran.

To make a long story short, Muawiya's representative presented Ali's representative with a deal to end the matter. The deal was that if Ali's followers removed Ali from leadership, the others would remove Muawiya from his leadership. Muslims could then elect whomever they saw fit according to the Quran.

Ali's followers kept their promise and removed Ali from leadership, but Muawiya's representative did not keep his promise. Instead, he declared Muawiya to be the only leader for the Muslims.

PRINCIPLE: Deceit is acceptable if it helps you achieve the goals of Islam.

MURDER OF ALI BY EL-KHARIJ

By A.D. 660 the Islamic world was divided into two parties—those who followed Ali and those who followed Muawiya. Ali's followers were the Shiites, and Muawiya's followers were the Sunni.

A new group splintered off from the Shiites. It was known as *El-Kharij*. Just like jihad groups today, El-Kharij called for reform. They wanted to practice Islam just as Muhammad did.

El-Kharij decided the best plan of action would be to kill them all—Ali, Muawiya and Muawiya's representative. By killing these three leaders they thought Muslims could go back to one leader, just as it was in the days of Muhammad.

One man was able to kill Ali even though Ali was held in great esteem among the Muslims. Immediately El-Kharij's spiritual leader claimed a Quranic passage to justify what they did (Surah 2:204, 207).

The murder of Ali is a leading example of what many radical groups believe.

PRINCIPLE: When a government or a leader is found acting not in accordance with the Quran, Muslims have the right to declare them renegade and infidel. Islam's way of dealing with a renegade or infidel is killing.

This is anther root of terrorism in the Islamic history.

El-Kharij principles and beliefs have been a terrorism threat to every empire, dynasty, society or nation since then. The Islamic militia groups that we see today around the world are a continuation of El-Kharij. Because this ancient group was so influential, let's look at their beliefs.

EL–KHARIJ BELIEFS

El-Kharij is an Arabic word that means "one who goes out." In this part of Islamic history, El-Kharij stepped out from under a leader or a government that they believed was not acting according to God's law and the Quran.

Here are some of their core beliefs:

- They believed that there is no law but God's law. They declared many imams (prayer leaders or Muslim preachers) to be infidels, including some of Muhammad's friends.

- They expected all Muslims to obey the call of jihad against rulers (Muslim or non-Muslim) who did not comply with the Quran. Anyone who did not participate in jihad was labeled an infidel.

- They believed in the right to kill children and women of infidels.

- They believed Muslims have the right to and control

over women, children and all material possessions
of infidels.

● They made assassination, dishonesty, mistrust and
unfaithfulness a strong part of the Islamic faith.

Their beliefs have been demonstrated throughout the history of Islam.[2]

SUICIDE MISSION BY MUHAMMAD'S GRANDSON

After Muawiya's death in A.D. 680, his son Yazid assumed the
leadership of the Islamic empire. As would be expected, he
was not accepted by Ali's son, al-Husayn, who was leader of
the Shiites at this time.

Al-Husayn felt that he should be the next leader of the
Islamic empire. Not only was his father Muhammad's right
arm and first cousin, but also his mother was Muhammad's
daughter.

Al-Husayn knew that he didn't have enough people or
weapons to defeat Yazid. However, he went to Iraq to fight
him anyway. Al-Husayn was killed in a city called Kabala in
the same year his father died.

The Shiites learned a new principle from the death of
their leader.

**PRINCIPLE: Fighting evil is a must; it does not matter if you
win or you die. If you win, you will be honored by victory;
if you die, you will be honored by God. Fighting evil is
an honor either way.**

Based on this belief, al-Husayn was a martyr of Islam. To
this day he is held in high esteem and as a great example of

self-sacrifice, especially among Shiite Muslims.

These beliefs give us a deeper understanding of why Muslims are willing to volunteer for suicidal attacks. They may not change much of the situation, but they get the opportunity to die as martyrs and heroes of Islam.

MARIJUANA WARRIORS

The name of this eleventh-century group is an Arabic description of people who smoke or eat hashish (derived from marijuana). *El-Hashashen* was a group of very religious Shiite Muslims who believed killing the enemy was an Islamic command to be martyred. This group was established in the eleventh century by a man named Hassan El-Sabaah.

Soldiers of this group used the drug hashish to get high before they went on suicide missions. While they were under the influence of the drugs, they visualized themselves in a garden with a many beautiful women. In their drug-altered states, they got a little taste of what heaven would be like, so they rushed to do their jobs and get to the real thing. Remember, we are talking about a movement from the eleventh century, but you can easily see its effect still today.

This movement grew quickly and accomplished a great number of assassinations and murders all over Persia and Iraq. The members of this group assassinated many military leaders and government officials of the Sunni Muslims. In the beginning of the twelfth century, the El-Hashashen movement almost took over the entire Middle East region. Not one ruler or governor was safe from their harassment.

IBN TAYMIYAH AND NO TOLERANCE

At the beginning of the fourteenth century a powerful Sunni leader came on the scene—Ibn Taymiyah. Born in a Syrian city named Haran in 1263, he fought the Mongolian invasion of Syria (1299–1303). Ibn Taymiyah taught that Mongolian Muslims were not true Muslims and that his countrymen should not submit to their authority. He also declared that anyone who submitted to them, helped them or dealt with them was just like them—infidels. From this point on Ibn Taymiyah acted as if he were a military leader, declaring many Muslims to be infidels and attacking them.

Ibn Taymiyah established the mind-set of no tolerance. He reinforced principles that were also practiced centuries earlier.

PRINCIPLE: Muslims should resist, fight and overturn any Islamic government that doesn't govern the land according to the Islamic law only.

PRINCIPLE: Muslims should enforce jihad on anybody whose beliefs differ from Islam, especially Jews and Christians.

We have seen a great deal of Ibn Taymiyah's influence for the last two centuries on most of the Islamic movements. Today's terrorism is a result of this mind-set.

WAHHABI MOVEMENT

Based on the same foundation that Ibn Taymiyah established, Muhammad ibn Abd al-Wahhab (1703–1792) led the Wahhabi movement. This movement resisted, fought and overturned the Turkish government. Abd al-Wahhab established a new 100 percent Islamic nation, which eventually became Saudi Arabia.

Today the leadership of Saudi Arabia is comprised of many members of the original movement. At the same time, the Saudi government is also facing an El-Kharij movement, those who would like to go back to the original principles. Osama bin Laden is an example of that group.

Ibn Taymiyah's mind-set has influenced our world today in a great way. Many movements are now trying to overturn their governments and go back to the teaching of Muhammad with no tolerance or compromise. They are pursuing their mission with military force. History is definitely repeating itself.

SUMMARY

Now that you have seen the historical roots of terrorism starting with Muhammad and going through the 1800s, we come to the man I refer to as the founding father of modern jihad. He was put to death by the government of Egypt for his teaching, and many of his books are banned in Egypt and other countries, including Libya and Iraq. Yet his influence lives on. His name is Sayyid Qutb.

The Founding Father
of Modern Jihad

Sayyid Qutb:
From the Village to the Gallows

T HE 1920s WERE an exciting time in the history of
many Middle Eastern countries. Many were finally
liberated from the authority of the Europeans—some
from the British, some from the French, some from the
Italians and some from the Turkish—or they were on their
way to liberation. One of these countries was Egypt.

For first time in history Egypt had a president. The people
of Egypt were finally starting to see the light of freedom
again, many for the first time in their lifetimes.

Events in Turkey would soon propel Egypt toward Islamic
fundamentalism. In 1924 the Turkish military leader
Mustafa Kemal Ataturk established a thoroughly secular
state in Turkey. In doing so, he overturned the Islamic succession system that had led the Islamic world for six hundred
years. In effect, he threw out the Muslim system and
replaced it with a Westernized, military system.

Muslims reacted negatively to this, including Muslims in
Egypt. In response, a spiritual leader named Sheikh Hassan

al-Banna started the Muslim Brotherhood Movement in Egypt. This is what we will refer to as El-Kharij all over again. His beliefs were a mixture of early El-Kharij, El-Hashashen and the mind-set of Ibn Taymiyah. His goal for Egypt was to reapply the Islamic law and to reestablish an Islamic succession system.

The Muslim Brotherhood was very militant, aggressive and full of hatred toward the leadership of the country and anyone who would not comply with Islamic law. They used terrorist methods to shake up society and pursue their agenda of bringing back the original glory of Islam.

After Israel was established as a nation in 1948, radical fundamentalist groups flourished even more. The establishment of Israel marked the beginning of many wars between the Jews and the Arabs.

The fundamentalist groups created many cells of rebellious, hateful Muslims who were willing to die for their cause. Their animosity was not directed at the Jews alone. They taught their followers that the leaders of Egypt and the rest of the Arabic world were not true Muslims.

They aggressively taught that Islamic law should be applied with zero tolerance for government interference or for people of any other faith. These militant and extreme terrorist groups focused their activities on assassination. In their minds, killing was the only way to make Islamic nations resubmit to the Quran and the Islamic law.

In 1948 the Muslim Brotherhood assassinated Egyptian Prime Minister Mahmoud Nokrashy Pasha. In 1949 they attempted the assassination of the new prime minister of Egypt, Abrahem Abd El-Hadi, but instead they killed Supreme Court Judge Moustashar Ahmad El-Kazendari.

Into this situation, Sayyd Qutb was born in Southern

Egypt in 1906. He earned a degree and became one of the top people in Egypt's department of education. In 1948 he was chosen by the government to come to the United States to study special methods of education and curriculum. After he returned to Egypt from his trip to the United States he joined the Muslim Brotherhood movement.

Sayyid Qutb, the "Martin Luther" of the modern jihad movement, put to death by the Egyptian government because of his book *Signs Along the Road.*

(Courtesy of Sinai Publishing, Cairo, Egypt)

VISITING AMERICA— AND HATING IT!

This was Qutb's first time ever outside of Egypt. He came back from America filled with both envy and hostility toward the United States. The following is a quote from a letter he sent to a friend while in the United States.

> Nowhere else on earth could I find people that excel in education, knowledge, technology, business and civilization like the Americans. However, the American values, ethics and beliefs are below the standard of a human being.

When Qutb was in the United States he spent time in Washington, D.C., California and Colorado. He was very impressed by America's natural beauty, great size, educational institutions and diversity of population. Yet he felt that America's resources were wasted on materialism.

> It seems to me that there is no relation between great-ness of culture and greatness of the people that create this culture. It is obvious that Americans have focused all of their ingenuity on the production of materialism, but they don't have much to offer as to what makes humans great.

He was disgusted with what he saw as a lack of religious conviction.

> No one else in the world has built more churches than the Americans . . . You will find Americans in church on Sundays, Christmas, Easter and special religious occa-sions, yet they are so empty and do not have a spiritual life. The last thing that an American would think about in everyday life is their religion.

Qutb was also angry because American influence had led the Muslim world astray from the ways of Islam.

> Not only the non-Muslim world is pagan and heathen but also the existing Muslim world is so influenced by the rest of the world.[1]

QUTB'S KEY BELIEFS

Sayyid Qutb, the founding father of modern jihad, authored more than seven books. However, the book that earned him a death sentence from the Egyptian government at the age of fifty-nine can only be found on the black market. The name of that book is *Signs Along the Road (Ma'alim fi el-Tareek)*. The Egyptian government arrested Qutb and sentenced him to death in 1965 during the presidency of Gamal Abdel Nasser. The Egyptian government thought that by killing Qutb they could stop the mind-polluting philosophy he taught.

The Egyptian government ordered the police to take into custody and burn any copies of his book; however, copies survived. I read this book in Egypt before I left. The book's contents continue to be distributed through the radical Muslims in Egypt and throughout the Islamic world.[2]

Signs Along the Road, the book that earned Qutb the death sentence but continues to guide jihad movements today.

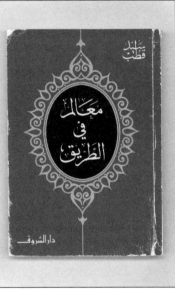

(Courtesy of Shorouk International, Cairo, Egypt)

Sayyid Qutb and *Signs Along the Road* have become the heartbeat of the radical Islamic movements of today. Some of the better known groups in Egypt that follow his teaching are *al-Jihad, El Takfir wal-Hijra* (Repentance and Holy Flight), *El Najune Min El-Narr* (Rescued from Hell) and many other terrorist groups. Qutb is the philosopher and spiritual leader of today's Islamic terrorist groups.

Let's take a closer look at Qutb's beliefs.

Qutb felt that the world had regressed to the way it was before Muhammad's teachings—pagan and idolatrous.

> Today we are living like heathens—just like the days
> before Islam in the way people act, the world's culture

and what they believe and think. It is all heathenism. Even in the Islamic world, Muslims' education, their philosophies, their culture, their thinking and their laws are all far from the true Islam.[3]

Qutb believed that Allah is the only ruler over earth and that no human should rule or govern the earth. Therefore, he rejected all man-made systems of government, including democracy, socialism, dictatorship and communism. He wrote:

> The way that life is lived today is an insult to Allah and his authority on earth. It contradicts godly principles. This idolatrous world gives the authority of Allah to humans as if they were God. We have become our own gods. These heathens are not like the ones before Islam, but far worse. Today's heathens reverence and honor man-made constitutions, laws, principles, systems and humanistic methods. They disregard Allah's law and his constitution for life.[4]

Qutb believed Muslims should rebel and resist any human power on earth until they overturn all man-made governments. This is the ultimate calling for a Muslim, and it is not to be compromised, deviated from or stopped.

> We should immediately eliminate this pagan influence and the heathen pressure on our world. We must overturn this current society with its culture and leadership of infidels. This is our first priority: to shake and change the foundations of heathens. We must destroy whatever conflicts with true Islam. We should get out from under the bondage of what keeps us from living in the ways that Allah wants us to live.[5]

His logic was: Good and evil cannot live together, truth and false are not the same, and people cannot live under the authority of both man and God. And to please God they should destroy the ways of man. He wrote:

> Demolish all governments and organizations that are established by man. Eliminate human racism that exalts one over the other. The return of God's kingdom can only be established by a movement of power and the sword.

Qutb, following the teaching of Ibn Taymiyah, went as far as declaring some Islamic leaders to be renegade infidels. He felt that this declaration gave him support from other Muslims and from Allah.

Qutb not only applied these methods within his country, but he also called the movement to enforce his beliefs all over the world.

PROFILE OF A JIHAD GROUP

Qutb brought the reader to an important question: How can this revolution be accomplished? He did not specify exactly what should be done to accomplish this. Perhaps he feared the Egyptian government would see this book as a plan for a new Islamic revolution to overturn their government.

Or perhaps he feared the government would be angry with him because his thinking was so similar to Sheikh Mawlana Abul Ala Mawdudi, the leader of the Islamic movement in Pakistan. (This is the author whose words I used earlier to define jihad.).

Another possibility could be his usual hastiness to get his teachings and beliefs out without thinking things through.

However, an average reader who can read between the

lines would conclude that Qutb envisioned the following type of group to carry out the call of Islam.

- This group would be purified from any and all inclination to lean toward the pagan world. They would eliminate all sources of spiritual beliefs that would compete with Allah and the Quran. This includes destroying books and man-made Islamic commentaries.

- They would accept no authority but Allah for beliefs, worship, systems, laws and constitution.

- They would experience tremendous resistance from the rest of the world. Existing governments and authorities would cause them financial difficulties. Their families and society would reject them.

- They would claim that the new Islamic world could exist only if their group obtained a great deal of power and force to gain the respect and submission of the pagan world. They would use armed forces to overthrow governments, just as Muhammad did.

- There would be no mercy or compromise in this war.

- This Muslim group may have a difficult start, but as soon as true believers hear the call, the numbers will multiply to hundreds, thousands, tens of thousands and then throughout the world.

"DEFEATED" MUSLIMS

Qutb was very frustrated with Muslims who questioned the call to jihad as a command to be followed by all

Muslims of all time. Qutb asserted:

> The order in which Allah gave Islam to Muhammad was gradual and progressive to maximize positive results toward Islam. Many Muslims take the early verses of this progression of teaching out of context as if they are Allah's final and complete instructions. These Muslims strip Islam of its power and build their own theory on these verses.
>
> The results of this type of interpretation of Islam are Muslims who are living a defeated life spiritually and mentally. They are under the pressure of the hopelessness that they cannot spread Islam any longer.
>
> These people are only Muslims by name. They only have the title of Islam but not the power. They only fight to defend their beliefs.
>
> These are the same Muslims who like to carry the title of Islam without the responsibility of overturning the entire earth with all of its politics and earthly governments. These Muslims choose to compromise the message of Islam by not forcing high taxes on people who refuse the message of Islam.[6]

Qutb expressed deep frustration about the people whom he described as "defeated Muslims, spiritually and mentally." He complained about them distorting the meaning of jihad. "These Muslims write about jihad in Islam as just a spiritual jihad against evil." He said that the truth is:

> Islam is nothing but Allah declaring his liberation to the human race on earth from slavery. Allah declares his lordship over the entire earth. This means that Allah greatly protests all man-made government and

authorities. Absolute rebellion is a must against anything on earth that conflicts with Islam. We should eliminate and destroy with great power anything that stops Allah's revolution.[7]

WORDS BACKED BY ACTION

Following Qutb's philosophy, the Muslim Brotherhood attempted to kill Egyptian President Gamal Abdel Nasser twice—once in 1954 and once in 1965. These terrorists planted bombs in many different places of gathering. Bombs were planted in the Cairo Bab El-Kalk Court and many police stations. They murdered many Egyptian policemen.

To defend itself, the Egyptian government placed many of the leaders of these groups in prison. Many of them left the prison in their coffins without a trial. President Nasser ordered the guards just to shoot them.

Sayyid Qutb's execution by the Egyptian government elevated his writings to a level of great authority in the Islamic world. He is respected and known by radical Muslims all over the world. He is held in esteem by Muslims the same way John Calvin or Martin Luther is held in esteem by Christians. There were long-term effects not only in Egypt, but also in the entire world.

Chapter 16

The Philosophers of Jihad

More Books That Guide Today's Terrorists

THERE IS A pattern among the philosophers of jihad. An author will write a book outlining his ideas of jihad and how it should be carried out. He will gather a following. Then that author is put to death by the government of his own country. The dead author is a hero, and his books gain more power.

Then the next author comes along and builds on the same ideas, only making them more radical. After three or four of these cycles, we have the philosophy of jihad today that resulted in Al-Qaeda and the attack on the United States on September 11, 2001.

DR. SALAH SEREA: THE EGYPTIAN ISLAMIC LIBERATION MOVEMENT

Qutb's teaching and philosophy captured a large number of Muslims, though many of his followers were imprisoned at the time of his hanging. Following this period of time, a man named Dr. Salah Serea led a new radical movement called the Islamic Liberation Movement (*Hezb al-Tarir*). He based his movement on the mind-set of Qutb's teaching. His goal was to overturn the Egyptian government and declare a new Islamic nation. Let's look at what Dr. Serea had to say:

- Muslims are nothing but talk. They make commitments but do not follow through. Throughout the last few centuries, Islam changed from a religion of action to a religion of just talk.

- The priority of the Islamic nations should be to carry on the message of Islam and apply it internally and externally in all ways.

- Jihad should be enforced. It is the way of paying a price for what you stand for and keeping the message alive. It should be practiced inside the nation and carried out to the world.

- Our goal is find out the most effective way to overturn and destroy any governments that do not completely comply with Islamic law, including existing Muslim countries.

- We will establish a great Islamic nation that will stretch across the world. The only political system will be Islamic law.[1]

Serea felt that leaders of the Muslim world are corrupted because they enforce fasting and prayer but not jihad:

> Many of the rulers of the Islamic world today are people of prayer. They have built mosques. They have reinforced fasting and prayer, and they do whatever it takes to have the appearance of good Muslims. Their

ulterior motive is to gain popularity using the religious sincerity of the Muslims. Meanwhile they carefully keep true Islam away from the hearts of the people. They persecute anyone who stands for true Islam with physical violence. These rulers are infidels, and anyone who stands behind them or supports them is also an infidel.[2]

Dr. Serea continued to complain about what he saw as the corruption of the existing Islamic governments by saying that Islam is one of the laws they use to govern the land when it should be the only law used to govern. Dr. Serea stated:

They are building mosques, but they are also building places of secular entertainment. They are broadcasting the Quran and also music and dancing. They give to charities and are also gambling. What is popular among these Muslims is only the worship part of Islam, and they leave out jihad, the heartbeat of Islam. These Muslims carefully read the Quran daily, and many of them cry in their prayers, but they do not go out and carry on the mission of Islam through jihad. These are hypocrite infidels. They are the shame of Islam.[3]

Dr. Serea practiced what he preached. On April 19, 1974, Dr. Serea and his movement launched their offensive against the Egyptian government. They invaded a military training institute in Cairo, hoping to establish a base from which to overturn the government.

The Egyptian authorities responded with great force and arrested him and all of the members of his movement. In October 1975 the federal government of Egypt sentenced Dr. Serea and many of his followers to death; twenty-nine followers of the movement remained in prison.

Egypt and the Islamic world were just entering a new episode of terrorism and radical Islamic groups. Even before Dr. Serea was sentenced, a new radical group was birthed in Egypt.

SHOKRI MOUSTAFA

Al-Takfir wal-Hijra (Repentance and Holy Flight) was the next militant group to carry on the goals of Dr. Serea. Its founder was Shokri Ahmad Moustafa, who was from the same region of Egypt as Sayyid Qutb. Born in 1942, Shokri Moustafa was only twenty-four years old when Qutb, the father of modern jihad, was hanged. He was thirty-three years of age when Dr. Serea was sentenced to death.

Shokri Moustafa, put to death by the Egyptian government in 1977 for jihad activity.

Shokri Moustafa was clear on what his goals and priorities were. The following is what he stated before the Egyptian

(Courtesy of AP/Wide World Photos)

federal court in the session on November 7, 1977:

> My greatest priority, for which I am willing to pay whatever price is required to accomplish it, is to see a

true Islamic movement take off. I must find fertile ground to plant a great Islamic nation worldwide. I will revive Islam and bring it to its original state.

The danger that the Egyptian court faced with Moustafa was that he had a large number of members in his organization who would obey him at a moment's notice. Moustafa said:

Each member of our movement would be willing to sacrifice his own life to fulfill the responsibility that Allah has put on our shoulders. That responsibility is to spread the message of Islam across the earth and reinforce it with the sword. My group of people will fight with me to the end to accomplish the great mission.

Shokri Moustafa kept a journal of poems in his own handwriting that the court used in his conviction. (Poetry is deeply ingrained in Islamic culture.) In Moustafa's most popular journal *The Battle (El-Maalhamma)* we find the poem "Before the Flood," which was written in 1967. In it, Moustafa expressed his deep sorrow and frustration with the current Muslim existence. He told himself that he must prepare for the calling on his life and his mission, and in doing so he should prepare to meet Allah.

In another poem titled "Immigration" (*"El-Hejhera"*) we see his belief that everything on this earth is vanity and that he simply wants to accomplish his mission and leave this earth.

In another journal titled *Expectation (El-Tawaseemat)*, he asked, "Where is the mother of the villages?" This is what Mecca was called during the time of Islam. Mecca is the city where Muhammad was persecuted, so it is considered evil for doing that. Moustafa was saying that Egypt was the modern Mecca, the modern persecutor of Islam. He called Egypt the place that imports evil, blasphemy and error. "It is the country of infidels," he wrote.

Moustafa comforted himself by saying, "Just as Muhammad left Mecca and immigrated to Medina to establish the first Islamic nation, I too will mentally escape from Mecca to go to my Medina to begin again."

From Egypt Moustafa planned to start an Islamic nation that would go all over the world. First he planned on winning many people from his home country, which would be the foundation for building a worldwide Islamic nation. From this new foundation he would export Islam to the world.

One of Moustafa's most disturbing beliefs was that his quest to spread Islam would involve great tension between the East and the West, which would lead to a worldwide nuclear war.[4] He believed that most of the world would be destroyed during this war, but his followers would not be killed because they would hide in caves of remote, isolated mountains. After the desolation, his followers would emerge from the caves and inherit the earth and rule it by the sword.

He believed that the use of the sword as a primary weapon, as it was in the time of Muhammad, would come back as a result of all modern technology and existing weapons being destroyed in a nuclear war.

MOUSTAFA'S DEFENSE

Shokri Moustafa's movement wanted to make Qutb's philosophy a reality. The members of this organization planned to start by living in complete isolation from the society of heathen. They were planning to work hard to increase their numbers and prepare for the point of power that would enable them to overturn the government and establish an Islamic nation. They believed their mission would be accomplished in two phases:

- Phase I—The absolute destruction of the heathen world.

- Phase II—Muslims would inherit the earth and everything on it.

During the prosecution of Moustafa, the Egyptian court asked him from what source he drew his philosophy. Moustafa replied, "It is from the clear-cut source of the Quran and Allah's word. We don't know anything, but Allah knows everything. We must learn only from Allah, and Allah only speaks from the Quran." He based this on the Quranic verse:

> Allah knows but you do not know.
> —SURAH 2:216, *THE NOBLE QURAN*

Any books other than the Quran are not acceptable.

Moustafa explained that this was what Allah said, and he asked the Egyptian Islamic authority if they were going to reject what the Quran says.

Shokri Moustafa and his organization were on trial for the kidnap and murder of a professor at Al-Azhar University—Dr. Husein El-Thehaby, one of the icons of the university. He was targeted because he led a team of professors to condemn and stop Moustafa's movement. Moustafa considered him to be an enemy of Allah and one of the infidels who were taking the side of the government.

Addressing the Egyptian court, Moustafa said that because Dr. El-Thehaby sold out to the pressure of the Egyptian government and compromised Allah's word to please man, they had carried out Allah's judgment against this renegade infidel.

Shokri Moustafa's movement gained more ground after a meeting between the Egyptian media and a new team from

Al-Azhar University. Dr. Sayed El-Tawhel, a professor of Islamic studies at Al-Azhar, led this new team, which advised, "Don't judge this group. They are sincere Muslims who just want to bring back the glory of Islam. We just need to sit down and talk with them." This statement was to clarify the air in Egypt and stop the confusion about a media broadcast that said Moustafa's organization was trying to spread a new Islam that was not based on the Quran.

The main Egyptian newspaper issued a statement from Dr. Tawhel, warning Al-Azhar University authorities not to issue any statements or judgments in the name of Islam against Moustafa. He called them to go back to the Quran and read it with new eyes; they would see that Moustafa's group was made up of sincere Muslims loyal to the call of Islam. Dr. El-Tawhel commended Moustafa and his group, saying that his heart's desire was to see more and more young people like them. He said that the Islamic world today needed people like them to lead it back to true Islam.[5]

THE EXECUTION AND THE BOOK

Shokri Moustafa was sentenced to death. He left behind a radical group that did not believe in any kind of submission, leadership or respect for the existing government in Egypt or the rest of the world.

His death confirmed to them that these governments were heathen. They believed every word when he said that these governments were infidels and any one who submits to them would be just like them.

Moustafa left behind a book with all of his beliefs and philosophies. The book is called *The Leader (Al-Kalafa)*. The Egyptian government confiscated every single copy that they could find and burned them. The actions of the government increased the value of this book among the followers of Muslim radical groups, which to this day continue distributing his beliefs and teaching.

Moustafa's new twist

This book was full of the mind-set of Qutb's teaching. The only new twist that made Moustafa more dangerous than Qutb is that he wanted to start by attacking religious institutes, police and military institutes. Moustafa explained that they should attack the religious institutes because they have submitted to the authority of a heathen government, which conflicts with Islamic law. He said to attack police and military institutes because they protect heathen governments and enforce their laws. The police and military institutes are the powers that persecute, imprison and kill true Muslims.

Shokri Moustafa appearing before the Egyptian court.

Moustafa's book declared there was not much difference between the existing governments of Israel, the United States and European countries. They are all heathen and the enemy of Allah according to Moustafa, and they should be fought through jihad until they submit to Islam completely.[6]

(Courtesy of Sinai Publishing, Cairo, Egypt)

In 1977, when the Egyptian government carried out the death sentence on Moustafa and some of his leadership, they were thinking that it would be the end of the movement. This was not the case. Radical groups flourished in Egypt in the 1970s and 1980s due to a variety of reasons. It was all leading to another attempt to overthrow the government.

Recruiting for Holy War

Terrorist Group Controls Egyptian Universities

I N THE EARLY 1970s the Egyptian government released many of the members of the Muslim Brotherhood Movement from the prisons. President Sadat thought that their activity would counterract the influence of the Soviets and communism in Egypt, which it did. But at the same time, the movement expanded, gained power and became dangerous to the Egyptian government as well.

A new group called *al-Gama'a al-Islamiyya*, known as the Islamic Group Movement, or IGM, in English, was formed. Its strategy was to recruit and disciple young men from the high schools and colleges.

Many of the older generation that were released from the prisons worked as mentors for the new generation. These mentors were former professors from Al-Azhar University.

RECRUITING AT MY UNIVERSITY

When the new Islamic Group Movement started, its leaders followed the first two steps of Qutb's plan. They started camps all over to prepare their members spiritually and mentally. They filled their camps with recruits from the universities of Egypt. These groups had complete control of the campuses of the major universities in Egypt.

The routine of the camps was for new members to come in for three to seven days to pray, fast and study the Quran and the history of Islam. They focused their study on Muhammad's life and how he led jihad and applied the Islamic law. The leaders of these groups brainwashed the students to believe that they were the only hope of Islam and that it was the time to get Islam back on the right track toward establishing an Islamic nation worldwide.

At the time I was living in Al-Azhar dorm in Nasser City in Cairo. This dorm had thirty-five hundred students from all over the country.

The Islamic Group Movement members utilized the campus mosque for their daily prayers, and in between prayers they worked hard to recruit and disciple new students into the movement. One day we were all at the mosque for prayer when an IGM leader stood up and said, "There is a secret Christian group that rents apartments near the dormitories. They are against Islam, and they are forcing female students to have sex with Christian men." Then he gave them the apartment numbers. The students were shocked and emotionally boiling.

He continued, "There is also a little shop near the entrance to the girl's dormitory. It is selling pens, paper and snacks. This shop is distributing pornography magazines for free to the Muslim girls. This Christian group is trying to get the girls out of Islam."

A fire was lit in the heart of every student. "Christians! Doing this to our girls? We will go and destroy them!"

Hundreds of students stampeded to the shop. They doused it with gas and burned it to the ground. Then they went to the apartments and destroyed them, too.

The mob of students returned to the dorm at lunchtime but refused to eat. They destroyed thirty-five hundred meals and kicked the workers out of the building. Then they locked the doors and rioted, running around the building shouting, "*Allah o akbar!*" (Allah is great!)

For three days the dormitory was locked down. There was no eating, no going to classes. But some students did not support this movement. To escape, they had to scale the wall around the dormitory and run back to their homes. I was one of those students. The standoff did not end until the president of the university and a government secretary met with the leader of IGM at the university.

Later, the minister of national security came to campus and declared that no Christian group was seducing the female students. This helped many students to recognize that groups like the IGM were just violent people who were trying to create an enemy to fight. They just wanted to show their power to society.

SPIRITUAL LEADERSHIP

Once a year the movement organized national rallies. The different university campuses united to hear people like Sheikh Abed Al-Hamid Kashk, Sheikh Omar Abdel Rahman or other leaders and icons of Islam to inspire the movement. Year after year this movement spread its wings over Sudan, Tunisia, Algeria, Yemen, Syria, Iraq, Lebanon and many other countries.

Sheikh Kashk and Sheikh Abdel Rahman made an incredible impact on the minds of the young men during that time.

Sheikh Abed Al-Hamid Kashk

Sheikh Abed Al-Hamid Kashk was one of the most eloquent leaders of Islam in Egypt and the Arab world. Sheikh Kashk had a very aggressive voice and special talent of utilizing the old classical Arabic language to hold the audience in the palm of his hand. He used his talents to deliver many political messages to thousands of young, thirsty minds. He controlled the minds of the audience almost like magic; he made them cry and laugh in the same breath.

Kashk was well known for his impudent and sassy tongue, and he attacked the government and those in high positions many times. Sheikh Kashk used cassette tapes to invade the Arabic world, breaking all the geographic barriers with his radical messages.

Sheikh Omar Abdel Rahman

Sheikh Abdel Rahman was my professor for "freshman Quran" at Al−Azhar. He is now serving a life sentence in the U.S. for the 1993 bombing of the World Trade Center. But you must recognize that before he came to the United States, he had an even greater impact on the Middle East.

A graduate and a professor of Al-Azhar University, he has his doctorate of philosophy in interpretation of the Quran and Islamic law. Sheikh Abdel Rahman became the spiritual authority and leader for today's radical groups.

His leadership was the perfect model for these radical terrorist groups as seen in the following characteristics:

● He did not compromise the Quran.

● He did not have any relationship with the government and did not submit to its laws and authority.

● He was a teacher of the Quran and Islamic law, which made many young Muslims trust him and obey his commands, even to kill.

● He led jihad according to the Quran and believed in building an Islamic nation according to Islamic law. He was willing to give his life for the cause.

While these two men were recruiting and building support to overturn Egypt, another nation in the Middle East finally succeeded. It would provide inspiration and support for many radicals. This country was Iran.

Chapter 18

Inspired by Iran

A Truly Islamic State Is Born

IN 1979 IRANIAN Shiite Muslims started their Islamic movement. They were against Muhammad Reza Shah Pahlavi and his government. The spiritual leaders of the country supported this movement to overturn the government.

Prior to this time, fundamentalist Iranian Muslims did not express their beliefs. They were in tremendous fear of the government. They followed the *Al-Tokiya* method of hiding their faith: "Inside I hate you, but outside I pretend to be your friend." *Al-Tokiya* meant that the Muslims behaved in a way that pleased the government, not according to their beliefs.

The rebellion started after many of the Shiite Muslims regained the spirit of martyrdom that was buried inside of them. They remembered how al-Husayn, the son of Ali ibn Abi Talib and the grandson of Muhammad, went to fight his enemy even though he knew he would be killed. The Iranian spiritual leaders reminded the Shiites of the history of martyrdom. Immediately Iranian Muslims started to abandon *Al-Tokiya* and to adopt the spirit of Shiite martyrdom.

At the same time and from a distance, Ayatollah Khomeini was leading this movement through cassettes. From a French village called Le Château, Khomeini recorded on cassette tapes his teaching, beliefs and plan for the new Islamic revolution and sent them to the people of Iran. These cassettes brainwashed millions of people. An Italian writer wrote a book about the Iranian revolution and called it *The War of Cassettes*.

Thousands of Iranians were killed in this revolution. Iranian history had never recorded such a powerful revolution before.

The revolution overthrew the government and succeeded in establishing an Islamic government. Ayatollah Khomeini was flown from France back to Iran. He bowed down twice outside the aircraft before the flight to Tehran and thanked Allah. Through reporters and media, he sent a message to the Shiites in Iran and to the world that "no one can defeat a nation that receives Allah's orders and obeys them."

Millions of Iranians received him at his arrival at Tehran's airport. The city was shaken by the sound of them shouting, "*Allah o akbar!*"—Allah is great. They carried Khomeini on their shoulders all the way to a graveyard called *Al-Ferdose*, where all the martyrs of the revolution were buried. Khomeini stated, "No more *Al-Tokiya* after today." He meant that the Shiite Muslims now had the power to practice their beliefs with no fear of a government or any other power in this world.

REACTION AT THE UNIVERSITY

Those historical days had a great impact on Islam and the world. At the university, members of the Islamic Group Movement used what happened in Iran to rebel against the

Egyptian government. They violently protested classes in all universities in Egypt, including Al-Azhar University.

Thousands of students shouted out in support of Khomeini. This protest included great numbers of students who had never been a part of the Islamic Group Movement before. This occasion was a great opportunity for new recruits.

The protest snowballed out of control throughout Egypt. The number of the protesters grew to be a major threat to the Egyptian authorities.

The Islamic Group members led thousands to shout against the government. They declared that Islam should take over Egypt, just like in Iran. "Oh Sadat, oh you coward, you are the puppet of the Americans," they shouted.

They cried out against the nation of Israel, too: "Patience, patience, all ye Jews: Muhammad's military is on their way back to you."

IRAN EXPORTS ITS REVOLUTION

The Iranian revolution supported many Islamic radical groups in the Arab nations and around the world. The leadership of the Iranian revolution said that they were getting into a new business. They were going to export their best product to the entire world—true Islamic law and revolution.

In the years since the revolution, Iran has supported all of the Islamic fundamentalist groups that have terrorized the world. One of the earlier groups that Iran planted and supported was Hizbollah. This was a Shiite group in Lebanon whose mission was to overturn the government there and establish an Islamic nation. Lebanon was a country that was led by the Christian majority.

Iran also supported the establishment of the Islamic nation in Sudan. Hasan al-Turabi, the leader of *Al-Jepha Al-*

Islamia, overturned the Sudanese government and established an Islamic nation there. Iran's support of Islamic movements traveled across many countries, including Egypt, Algeria, Tunisia and many other Arab countries.

IRAQ STRIKES IRAN

Fear and terror struck the Arab countries of the Gulf. They were threatened by the Iranian project of exporting revolution into their countries. Saddam Hussein, the ruler of Iraq, had no intention of sharing his authority with fundamentalist Muslims or anyone else. He led the regional defense against the Iranian revolution and invaded Iran. All the Arab countries and the rest of the world supported him.

The Iraqi military invaded 30 percent of the Iranian homeland. The Iranians took advantage of this opportunity to defend their home and become martyrs in the name of Allah. It took two years of war for the Iranians to kick the Iraqi military out of their land. The Iranians did not stop at the border. They took the war into Iraqi soil for six more years.

The Iran/Iraq war killed almost one million Muslims from both sides, and two million were wounded. This war was intended to slow down Iran's project of exporting their movement to the Arab countries. However, the mission became stronger, and the project of spreading Islam to the world never stopped.

The Iranian revolution sent a new hope to all Islamic movements in the world. That new hope was that Islam would take over the earth and lead the world.

Chapter 19

Treachery Between Terrorists

Egypt's Militant Fundamentalists Nearly Self-Destruct

IN 1980 A situation was developing in Egypt that would cause a great setback to those pursuing jihad. The Egyptian leaders of the Islamic Group Movement (IGM) felt that they should get out of the spiritual and mental preparation time and make the move to overturn the Egyptian government. They also believed it was time to join with Sudan and Iran (who had already established Islamic states) and get the invasion of the Arab world completed so that they could move on to the worldwide vision.

The IGM divided Egypt into regions and assigned strong leaders to each region. Those regions and their leaders were:

- Al-Minya region: Karm Zohdi, Fouad Al-Dolabi, Assim Abdul-Majed, Ayman al-Zawahiri (later he became the right-hand man of Osama Bin Laden) and Essam Driya

- Asyut region: Najeh Ibrahim and Osama Hafez

- Sohaj region: Hamdi Abdul Rahman

- Nagh Hamadi region: Ali Sharif and Talat Qusam

All of these regional leaders were led by General Prince Halmmi Al-Gazar and his assistant, Essam Al-Aryan.[1]

A MOVE TO JOIN THE TWO GROUPS

This newly organized Islamic Group Movement was a threat to the leadership of the Muslim Brotherhood. Omar Al-Talmasani, the leader of the Muslim Brotherhood Movement, also disagreed with the timing of their plans. He told all Muslims, "It is not the right time for jihad yet." He advised the leaders of the Islamic Group Movement (IGM) to learn some patience, not hastiness.

He also declared it was not good for the unity of Muslims to have two different movements. He suggested that they should unite under his leadership so that they could be more effective.

The leader of IGM, his assistant and the Al-Minya region leaders immediately welcomed the call for unity, claiming the Quranic verse. "Verily, Allah loves those who fight in His Cause in rows (ranks) as if they were a solid structure" (Surah 61:4, *The Noble Quran*). He said this verse spoke of the unity that Muslims should have.

The IGM leadership invited the leader of the Muslim Brotherhood to go to the southern region of Egypt to have the ceremony of unity. However, many other members of the IGM disagreed with the call for unity. As soon the delegation from the Muslim Brotherhood arrived, a storm of rage swept through the IGM members. Those who rejected the idea of unity attempted to attack the leader of the Muslim Brotherhood. The members who were for unity defended him by killing the fellow members that disagreed.

TERRORIZING FELLOW MUSLIMS

What followed was a war between civilians fought with knives and swords. The Egyptian citizens who lived in the regions of Asyut and Al Minya lived in terror of this conflict. Members of the group who opposed unity went to their fellow members' homes and knocked on the doors. When the doors were opened, they stabbed the people of the house to death. Before the victim breathed his last breath he was told he was a betrayer of Allah and Islam; therefore, he was receiving the punishment of whoever delayed jihad as stated by the Quran.

Many times the IGM members of the house were not home, but this did not stop the attackers. They slaughtered the wives and children, telling them the same message. Hundreds of members took trains from all over the country and came to this troubled region to stop the rage and save their movement.

Through bloodshed and terror, IGM members who opposed unity took over. They submitted the remainder of both movements to their authority. This bloody storm almost wiped out the IGM.

AL-JIHAD IS BORN

Out of IGM, the Muslim Brotherhood and other smaller groups, a new splinter group called *al-Jihad* emerged. It was led by Mohammed Abdul-Salam Farag. In the mid-1980s they accomplished a number of murders, including the murders of philosophers, journalists and the head of the Egyptian Parliament.

(Courtesy of Sinai Publishing, Cairo, Egypt)

Egyptian al-Jihad leaders appearing in court: (from left)
Tarek al-Zomor (25-year sentence) and Abod al-Zomor
(40-year sentence).

Al-Jihad in Egypt was greatly advanced by a chance meeting that occurred when Farag visited the home of one of the movement's members, Tarek Al-Zomor. At the time, Zomor was also hosting his brother-in-law, who was a high-ranking Egyptian military intelligence officer (Abod Al-Zomor).

(Courtesy of Sinai Publishing, Cairo, Egypt)

Egyptian al-Jihad leaders appear in court: (from left)
Assim Abdul-Majed (40-year sentence), Abod al-Zomor
(40-year sentence), Karm Zohdi (40-year sentence) and
Hamdi Abdul Rahman (15-year sentence).

There was a real bonding among these three men. They vowed to each other to do whatever it would take to overturn the Egyptian government and liberate Egypt from renegade and infidel leadership.

This took place in the summer of 1980. Abod Al-Zomor said, "I wished many times to step out from under the government's authority and start fighting the government. Now, after meeting Farag, we got likeminded to organize the right plan to establish the goal of the Islamic government."

Soon after that historical meeting took place, the leaders of al-Jihad (Abod Al-Zomor, Karm Zohdi, Fouad Al-Dolabi and Nabil Al-Magrabi) met to organize the movement and set up an operating system. After long discussions they decided to have a committee of counselors.[1]

The committee agreed to focus on appointing, managing and making the necessary decisions. They also agreed to spin off from the committee three minor committees:

- Preparation committee—its responsibility was to organize and prepare weapons and transportation.

- Economic committee—its responsibility was to raise the necessary finances to accomplish the mission.

- Distribution and awareness committee—it was in charge of preparing and distributing literature to those involved in upcoming jihad.

The committee of counselors divided the country into regions and set up the committee members as princes over these regions.[2]

The committee gave the right to all leaders to choose their own assistants for these regions. Each region was responsible for its own military training and funding. Now the movement of al-Jihad was truly a reality in Egypt. Later it would reproduce itself throughout the rest of the Islamic world.

The most well-known offspring is al-Jihad in Palestine. Its leaders were trained by Egyptian radicals, and you can see similarities in their methods. For example, al-Jihad in Egypt had two men strap bombs to their bodies and blow themselves up in an attempt to kill the Egyptian minister of national security. In the same way, al-Jihad in Palestine sends people on suicide missions

THE PHILOSOPHY OF AL-JIHAD

Al-Jihad was organized. Now it needed a strong philosophy to bind its members together. This philosophy was found in a book called *The Missing Commitments* (*Al-Fareda Al-Gaaba*) written by an engineer named Mohammed Abed al-Salem.

The author of this book met with the southern Egypt region's leader (Karm Zohdi), who made the book the by-laws of al-Jihad.

I would like to summarize the book, which is written in three chapters. The book emphasizes jihad as the only way for Islam to rise again. However, the author takes his book one step further than any other book by saying, "The Islamic invasion is coming to Rome." Previous Muslim writers had focused on the Arab world and some of the African countries; however, in this book al-Salem started talking about invading Europe and the West. Here are samples of al-Salem's opinions:

Compromised Muslims are condemned.

Fundamentalist Islamic authority must be established in

every nation—it doesn't make any difference whether Muslims like it or not. It is the command of Allah, and it must be done. Al-Salem said the crucial question to answer is this: "Are we living in a true Islamic nation?"

He questioned the leadership of many Muslim countries: "How can they be sincere Muslims? They were raised and influenced in Judaism, Christianity and Communism." He felt these leaders were Muslims by name only. He declared them all to be renegades, infidels and heathens who should be killed.

He also emphasized that the punishment should be harder on these Muslims than on the heathens. He agreed with fourteenth-century scholar Ibn Taymiyah and wrote, "Muslims should not mix with anyone else, and if they do, they should be killed as well."

Jihad supercedes other duties.

He condemned all other religious activities in Islam, such as fasting, prayer and charitable works because they keep Muslims so busy that they ignore the call of jihad.

Killing is the Muslim's responsibility.

Killing is the big difference between Islam and all other religions. Abed Al-Salem wrote that before Islam, Allah dealt with infidels and heathens sometimes with fires, sometimes with floods and sometimes with other ways. However, since the establishment of Islam, Allah commanded Muslims to take the law into their own hands; it became their responsibility to torture and kill the enemies of Allah.

Jihad is offensive, not defensive.

Abed al-Salem attacked the Muslims who believed that jihad was just to defend Islam. He aggressively emphasized that jihad is not negotiable—nor can it be compromised. Jihad is the call to all Muslims. To support his point of view, he gave examples of the prophet Muhammad's letters to the kings of countries, of how the early Muslims fought and of how Islam spread by the sword. He said that Islam should be spread this way today.

The enemy is redefined.

He also defined the enemies in a new way. They were:

● Heathens
● Muslims not governed according to Allah's law and the Quran

Abed al-Salem supported fighting those Muslims who did not live according to his interpretation of Islam.

War strategies are set in place.

Al-Salem allotted a large portion of his book to the Islamic methods of war and jihad: attacks, murders, deceit, perfidy, foul play, treachery and breach of faith. He also explained how women, children and all other material possessions of the enemy belong to the Muslims and their military; Muslims should exterminate anyone that fights back.

THE NEXT STEP

Al-Jihad had its foundation in place. Its hope was to follow the path of Iran and create the next truly Islamic state. Al-Jihad needed to raise funds, and its members decided to copy Muhammad's methods. In the next chapter, you will learn what they did.

Chapter 20

Al-Jihad Prepares
and Attacks

Christian Businesses Robbed to Raise Funds

A S AL-JIHAD PREPARED for war in the 1980s, they needed guns, bombs, weapons and transportation. They found themselves under tremendous pressure to come up with large sums of money. The Muslims were not committed enough to give this amount of support.

According to the Egyptian court records, an investigation found that the movement received a personal donation from Abod Al-Zomor of four thousand Egyptian pounds, several automatic machine guns, six tear-gas bombs, four RBG bombs, seven Russian bombs, Russian Kalashnikov guns and several hand guns. These were donated from his personal cache. But these donations and many others were not enough to support the movement. They had to find another source of support.

TERRORIZING THE CHRISTIAN MINORITY

A criminal Islamic solution was presented by Ali Sharif, the leader of Quna and Nagh Hamadi regions. He suggested that the movement should take the possessions of the Egyptian Christian minority (15–17 percent of the population) and use them for support. His idea was nothing new. The El-Kharij movement of the seventh century had the same philosophy: "Their women and all possessions are our rights." The idea went all the way back to Muhammad killing his enemies and plundering their cities.

This hellish idea created not a question of morality, but of execution–how? How can we get the Christian's possessions? Should we rob them, enforce the *jizyah* (special taxation for unbelievers) or use extortion? Should we target the possessions of the Christian citizens only or of the churches also?

The Christian citizenry dominated several different industries in Egypt, one of these being the production of gemstones and jewelry. The idea was to attack the businesses, kill the Christians and confiscate all money and merchandise.

After the committee heard this idea there was a long silence. The Asyut region leader, Najeh Ibrahim, broke the silence by saying, "This is nothing but a heavenly inspiration."

Then the Al Minya region leader, Karm Zohdi, added, "We should start with any business that supports the churches and their ministry." The committee agreed, and Ali Sharif became responsible to plan the first attack.

From the records of the court's sessions we can hear the testimony from one man who witnessed an attack:

> On July 26, 1981 at noon I was in the jewelry store of Nabih Massod Askaros, in the city of Nagh Hamadi. The owner, his workers and a few customers were in the store. I heard several shots at the door of the store.

> I immediately hid under a table. I saw two men carrying automatic machine guns. They were wearing face-masks and gloves. They fired at the owner and also at Zarif Shinooda. They took all of the merchandise and money and, while fleeing, continued firing their guns. In the meantime, I found out that they did the same thing to Fouad and his brother, Fayzi, Massod's jewelry store. Six men were killed and two were injured in that store. The two robbers got in a Peugot and took off.

The Christian community lived in great terror during this time because many were killed, and they wondered who would be next.

The court record indicates that the movement got a lot of support from Egyptian Muslims who worked in oil-producing countries. The donations that were discovered included 21,000 in dollars, 10,400 in German marks, 26,000 in Egyptian pounds and much more. All of this wasn't enough money, so they started stealing vehicles belonging to Christian church personnel. These vehicles were then transported to the desert, disassembled and sold as used parts so that the police would not be able to track them down.

Al-Jihad killed, robbed and stole from Christians as they were taught by the Quran regarding the People of the Book—Jews and Christians.

> Fight against . . . those who acknowledge not the religion of truth (i.e. Islam) among the people of the Scripture (Jews and Christians), until they pay the *Jizyah* [tax] with willing submission, and feel themselves subdued.
>
> —SURAH 9:29, *THE NOBLE QURAN*

The application of this verse would have been difficult in

Egypt because of the large Christian population—there were too many Christians to kill them all. However, this was still the movement's goal—to apply the Islamic law and force Christians to pay a high taxation to Muslims, or they would be killed.

Now al-Jihad was ready and able to go in for the first major confrontation with the Egyptian government and its system. They planned to overturn the system and submit Egypt to be the base of the worldwide Islamic nations' revolution.

During this time the committee of counselors added eleven new members, but they felt that they needed one man to lead them through this major historical operation. After much thinking they decided to elect Sheikh Omar Abdel Rahman, the professor of Quranic science that I sat under at Al-Azhar University. Though blind, he was more than capable of leading such a movement.

President Sadat Assassinated

Sheikh Abdel Rahman issued a *fatwa* that President Sadat and his government were renegade infidels who all must die.

The plan to overturn the country included these steps:

1. Kill the president.

2. Gain control over strategic places in Cairo, such as the defense department, national security department and the national radio and TV stations.

3. Take over the Asyut region in South Egypt and call the Muslim Egyptians to come out for a new Islamic revolution.

For their sharpshooter, al-Jihad commissioned Khaled al-Islambouli, who was a soldier in the Egyptian military and the national champion in long-range shooting. He was also an active member of al-Jihad.

Everything started out according to plan. On October 6, 1981, the president was shot and killed during an annual military celebration of winning the 1973 Israeli war. The Asyut region was in the hands of the movement, but they did not succeed in taking over Cairo.

After the assassination of Sadat, Vice President Mubarak immediately ordered the military to go and liberate the Asyut region from the movement's control. The government was able to arrest the leadership of al-Jihad, including Sheikh Omar Abdel Rahman. They all stood before Egypt's highest military court.

The question now was, How could the legal system in an Arabic, supposedly Islamic, country deal with these Muslims who obeyed the call of Islam according to the Quran? Let's look at the court record of perhaps the most crucial case in Egyptian history.

Justice Loses, Quran Wins

Sheikh Uses Quran
to Defend Assassination and Win Release

IT WAS SHEIKH Omar Abdel Rahman's moment to show his talents to the court.

He stood before the court to defend the philosophy of the al-Jihad movement. He had the floor twice—once to explain to the jury the mind-set of jihad, and once to respond to the questions of the attorney general. When you read carefully the court transcript and his answers, you will see Islam's true colors. Sheikh Abdel Rahman, the scholar of the Quran and Islamic law, put his expertise to work for the movement in a way that no one ever expected.

He led the attorney general to play the game that he mastered all of his life. He succeeded in turning the table of accusation and putting the attorney general on the defense. Sheikh Omar Abdel Rahman set the stage for himself in the first round. He made the following Islamic principles clear to the court:

Sheikh Omar Abdel Rahman appearing before the Egyptian Supreme Court after the assassination of President Anwar Sadat.

(Courtesy of Sinai Publishing, Cairo, Egypt)

- Justice should be according to what Allah has set for the Muslims only. Allah's lordship should be acknowledged by all Muslims, and no one can deny it because Allah created everything and everyone. He has the absolute right to his creation.

- The people who carry out Islamic justice should be faithful believers who obey Allah's commands and the prophet Muhammad's teaching. If the justice system is not run according to the Quran, Muslim believers should not submit themselves to its laws.

- The imported laws from infidel countries, "USA and Europe," are man-made and not according to Allah's laws. The existing law of Egypt is influenced by men who compromise Allah's law in many areas such as adultery, gambling, homosexuality, alcoholism and theft. Anyone who modifies Allah's laws is a renegade infidel. Anyone who submits to these laws is also a renegade infidel.

Sheikh Abdel Rahman established the authority of his

words by claiming, "What I'm saying is not opinion or one person's spiritual ideas, but it is what Allah's book says."

Following is a portion of the court transcript during the final court session, when the attorney general questioned the sheikh.

Attorney General:	In Islamic history we find many Muslims who claimed that Allah is the ultimate judge but acted any way they pleased. Islam called them *el-Kharij*. Islamic society rejects them.
Sheikh Rahman:	*Kharij* are those who rebelled against or disobeyed the Islamic successor, so who is the Islamic successor today? Where is Ali ibn Abi Talib today? And if you call us *Kharij*, it means that we disobeyed or rebelled from the successor, the Muslim leader. So who is today's successor and leader of Muslims? Is he the friend of Jews, the supporter of Israel and Begin's buddy? [He referred to peace talks between President Sadat, Menachem Begin, prime minister of Israel, and Jimmy Carter, U.S. president. Sadat was the recipient of the Nobel Peace Prize at this time.] Is our successor the man who abandoned Allah's law and commanded compliance with the laws of heathens and infidels?
Attorney General:	The belief that Allah is the lawmaker and the only judge does not mean that if our Islamic society finds solutions according to our social and mental standards of living today that so doing makes it a renegade, infidel society.

Sheikh Rahman:	Disobeying Allah and his law in the name of convenience has only one meaning—these are sinful, lost infidels who have made their own laws and abandoned Allah's laws. They are the ones whom Allah commanded the Muslims to kill in jihad.
Attorney General:	Jihad is not killing. This is not Islam's teaching. Jihad is a spiritual fight against evil, poverty, sickness and sin. Killing is only from the devil.
Sheikh Rahman:	From where does the attorney general come up with this understanding? Are there verses in the Quran that I don't know about that say jihad is a spiritual fight against evil, poverty, sickness and sin? Perhaps there is new inspiration from Allah that our attorney general received recently and the rest of the Muslims do not yet know.
Attorney General:	Declaring that our Islamic society is heathen, infidels or renegades is an insult on our merciful Allah, his commands and his law.
Sheikh Rahman:	Which commands and laws are you talking about? The ones that compromised adultery, gambling and alcohol? Is this not our merciful Allah's command? Mr. Attorney General, your commands and laws are from the devil.
Attorney General:	If any Muslim society confesses that Allah is the only God and Muhammad is his prophet, no one has the right to accuse them of being infidels.

Sheikh Rahman: What you say is not the real truth. Someone can confess that Allah is God and Muhammad is his prophet, but he can do something against his confession, and this takes him outside of Islam.

Attorney General: President Al-Sadat was a great man who sacrificed his life for the love of Allah and the love of his country.

Sheikh Rahman: Do you know how this man sacrificed his life for the love of his country? He is the same man who declared that all religions are equal. He made the infidels and the grandchildren of "monkeys and pigs" [*monkeys and pigs* is the description the Quran uses for the Jewish people] equal to the Muslims. He made the world's greatest criminal murderer his dear friend [referring to Begin, Israel's prime minister]. The same man who sacrificed his life for Allah broke all of Allah's laws in this country. The same man who worshiped Allah sarcastically described the Muslim women's veil as a tent. This man loved Allah? He also insulted Allah when he danced with and hugged women publicly before the international media and before the whole world. [In celebration of the peace agreement, Sadat and his wife danced with Carter and his wife on national television.] This contradicts what Sadat always preached about village behavior. This man led our country to free enterprise and nearly destroyed our economy. He led our country to a moral and social disaster, and it will take our country many years to recover from him.

You have witnessed, dear reader, how Sheikh Omar Abdel Rahman not only defeated the attorney general, but how he also defeated the justice system in Egypt.

Yes, jihad means killing all the enemies of Allah and Islam. Yes, Muslims believe in taking the law into their own hands and killing Allah's enemies, as if he can't handle them himself. Yes, the laws of the land could not overrule the Quran. Yes, the mastermind of the murder of the president could justify his acts through the Quran and be declared not guilty in the highest court of a great nation, Egypt. What a shame.

Sheikh Abdel Rahman was set free officially because they did not have material evidence that he was the one who gave al-Jihad the religious order to kill Sadat as an infidel. In my opinion, the blind sheikh's own words were more than enough evidence for a conviction.

However, the crime did not go unpunished. Five men were executed military style, including Khaled al-Islambouli, the sharpshooter, and Mohammed Abed al-Salem, the author of *The Missing Commitments*. When the police arrested the author, they confiscated all his books and burned them. It can only be found on the black market now.

In spite of the tremendous resistance of the Egyptian government, al-Jihad survived, grew and never stopped. Many of the leaders of the al-Jihad movement were able to flee to other countries, like Sudan, Yemen, Pakistan and Czechoslovakia. A large number went to Afghanistan to become a part of the al-Jihad movement there.

Later they united with Osama bin Laden, who based his movement on the same beliefs and principles. Those leaders who fled from Egypt, the original members of al-Jihad, helped bin Laden to establish a new movement. They named it al-Qaeda. Dr. Ayman al-Zawahiri, one of the Egyptian al-

Jihad leaders, became bin Laden's right hand man. Afghanistan became the place of refuge for those who were persecuted by the Egyptian government.

Khaled al-Islambouli, put to death by the Egyptian government in 1981 as the sharpshooter who assassinated President Anwar Sadat.

Later, the fundamentalist Islamic group in Afghanistan, the Taliban, welcomed all of these men and supported them as partners in the same call of jihad—ready to be partners in death but hoping to be the victors when Allah's people rule the world.

(Courtesy of Sinai Publishing, Cairo, Egypt)

World of Islam

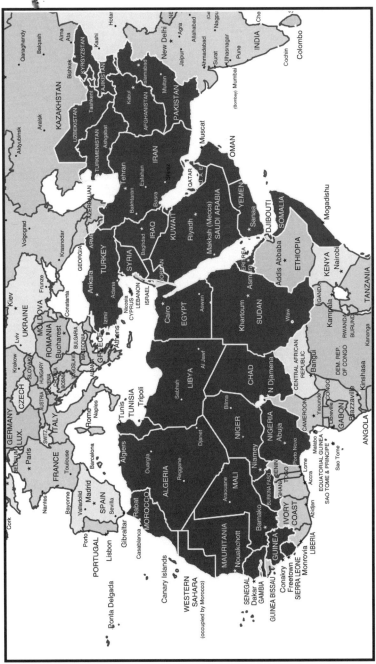

Chapter 22

Jihad Bleeds
Out of Egypt

*Egyptian Leaders Travel
to Surrounding Countries*

WHEN YOU THROW a stone into the water, the ripples go in all directions. This is what happens with militant fundamentalist groups. A major event in one country causes a ripple effect in many other countries.

Egypt is like the stone that was tossed into the water. It is at the center of modern terrorism. The reason for this is that Egypt is the capital of Islamic education for the entire world. Al-Azhar sends missionaries everywhere to spread Islam.

If there are religious questions in a Muslim nation anywhere in the world, they ask Al-Azhar. When I was in South Africa, if the Muslims had a question they couldn't answer, they wrote to Al-Azhar. For example, they needed a ruling on when to start Ramadan, which depends on the sighting of the new moon. Al-Azhar declared that when they could see the moon in Cairo, the world could start Ramadan.

At the time when Muslim Brotherhood, IGM, al-Jihad and others were developing, I was immersed in Al-Azhar University. I spent eleven years there, earning my bachelor's, master's and doctorate degrees. In addition, after I earned my bachelor's degree, the university sent me out as a visiting professor to Islamic universities in other countries, including Tunisia, Libya, Iraq and Morocco. From this vantage point, I observed what was happening.

We've looked in detail at the uprisings in Egypt and Iran. Now let's see the ripple effects of Sadat's assassination in North Africa. Going west from Egypt, the movement traveled to Libya, Tunisia and Algeria. Going south, effects were felt in Sudan.

LIBYA

Next door to Egypt, thousands of Libyan Muslim men were inspired by the murder of Sadat. They too were willing to die in the name of Allah and for the cause of jihad.

The Libyan Muslims have organized many movements to assassinate Muammar Qaddafi and overturn his government, yet they haven't succeeded.

Though Qaddafi is a Muslim, many Westerners may not recognize that his position is far from Islamic fundamentalism. After he took over in 1965, he ruled the country with a constitution, not Islamic law. His original goal was to create a democracy.

Qaddafi admired the past president of Egypt, Gamal Abdel Nasser, for his harsh methods for dealing with the Muslim Brotherhood Movement. (President Nasser was well known for his zero tolerance of radicals. Twice he gathered them and slaughtered them—in 1954 and 1965.) Qaddafi takes every opportunity to call radical Muslims "the street dogs" on Libyan national television. He follows Nasser's methods: He has slaughtered radicals many times to eliminate their influence in his country.

TUNISIA

The influence of the Egyptian al-Jihad traveled from Libya into Tunisia. It served as inspiration for the *Nahda Al-Islamia* movement and its leader, Rashet Al-Fenwsy. They were in constant struggle with the previous president Habib ibn Ali Bourguiba and now president Zine El Abidine Ben Ali.

I visited Tunisia in the early 1990s, and the Muslims treated me with great respect because I came from the country of Islamic heroes. They called Khaled al-Islambouli a modern Islamic hero for killing Sadat. They told me, "Our Islamic Arab nations need people like that to overturn all of the infidels' governments and establish the Islamic dynasty just as in Muhammad's days."

ALGERIA

To fully appreciate the effect in Algeria, we need to look at the unique history of this country. It was one of the first areas to be conquered by Islam.

Within ten years after the death of Muhammad, the Islamic military invaded Algeria. From that point on, Algeria remained an Islamic state under the Islamic empire until the French invaded it in 1830. The French occupied Algeria until 1962. The French influence was so strong in the Algerian culture that even after the liberation, French remained the main language; throughout most of the country the Arabic language was almost forgotten.

After the Algerian revolution that was led by Ahmed Ben Bella, Algeria was governed by a national government that was not Islamic based. Many Arab Muslim countries helped Algeria to overcome the French influence and establish

Islam and the Arabic language. My uncle was one of the head missionaries sent by Al-Azhar University to Algeria to teach the Arabic language and to reinstall Islam.

Slowly but surely, Algeria became an Arabic country again. In the process, Algeria was influenced by two major Egyptian organizations: Al-Azhar University's educational mission and the Muslim Brotherhood Organization.

During Egyptian president Nasser's tremendous persecution of the Muslim Brotherhood Organization between 1954 and 1960, many of its members immigrated to Algeria. They spread their beliefs among the new generation of Algerians.

Ali Belhadj and Dr. Abbas al-Madani, who were professors at the University of Algiers, started a new Islamic movement called *al-Gabha al-Aslamia Lilncaz*, meaning Islamic Salvation Front. This was just a new name for the Muslim Brotherhood of Egypt. This movement had a strong relationship with other Islamic movements across the Arab countries, especially Egypt.

The leaders of the Algerian and the Egyptian movements worked closely together to lead all Islamic movements in the world at the time. These two groups worked hard to enter Morocco, Tunisia and Libya to establish the Islamic nation across North Africa. They planned to unite with the movements in Sudan and Iran so that the world would see the reestablishment of the Islamic authority throughout the Arabic region.

Muammar Qaddafi immediately felt a threat to his government in Libya. He was pressured from the east by the Egyptians and from the west by the Algerians. Qaddafi volunteered to help the existing government of Algeria fight the radical groups and their leaders, al-Madani and Belhadj.

Hijacking an election

In the early nineties the leaders of the Islamic Salvation Front hosted one of history's largest rallies for Islamic fundamentalist groups. They jam-packed the national soccer stadium. The Algerian capital will always remember the crowd's cheers that day: "Allah is great! Patience, patience, all ye Jews; Muhammad's forces are on the way."

All of these anti-Jewish hate cheers were inspired by the guest speaker, Khaled al-Islambouli's mother. Yes, the mother of President Sadat's assassin, who was put to death by the Egyptian government, spoke to the leaders of jihad in Algeria.

During her speech she inspired the crowd to sacrifice their money as well as their souls to make jihad a reality in their country and the world. She stated that she gave one son as a sacrifice for jihad, and she was willing to present her other son, Mohammed, who was standing on stage beside her, to the same cause—to see the banner of Islam take over the world. She said that she was willing to die herself to bring victory to Islam over the enemy.

The crowds cheered aggressively when she said, "Nothing made me more proud as a mother than that my son Khaled was sentenced to death by the enemy of Islam." She ignited the spirit of jihad and martyrdom in everyone's heart when they heard her saying how many roads and streets were already named in honor of her son in Islamic nations around the world. She added, "Even the enemies of Islam look at my son as a hero for giving his life for what he believes in." She quoted one of the prophet Muhammad's teachings in hadith, "Any nation that abandons jihad will be conquered and subdued."[1]

Make no mistake; this woman left the crowd in the flames of hate toward their government. She prepared the

Algerian movement for what would happen in their battle to overturn the government. The impact of this rally was electrifying. It gave the Muslims in Algeria the courage to carry out their mission.

Not long after this rally, a new election was held (1991). The Islamic Salvation Front used this opportunity to manipulate the election for their personal gain, hoping to take over. The movement won the election by scaring all other candidates out of running for office; however, it was not going to take over the country that easily.

The Algerian upper class, the elites and the highly educated citizens immediately rose up to warn and object to the existing government turning over authority to these radicals. Many of the Arabic countries such as Egypt, Libya, Tunisia and Morocco were familiar with the danger of these groups. They also warned the government about the results of letting the radicals take over. Algeria had no other option but to order the military to secure the country and cancel the election. This was the beginning of the long battle between the military and the Islamic movement that continues to this day.

In the last six years, more than one hundred fifty thousand people have been killed to keep fundamentalist Islam from ruling their nation. The Algerian government arrested the leaders of the Islamic Salvation Front, but it could not stop the bloodshed. Afghanistan sent in many experienced fighters to try to unseat the government.

And the bloody struggle continues.

SUDAN

Sheikh Omar Abdel Rahman went south to Sudan after he was released from prison. He spent a few months there with Dr. Hasan al-Turabi, the leader of the Sudanese movement *al-Islamia*. Al-Turabi had succeeded in overturning the Sudanese government and taking over the country with the help of one of the generals of the Sudanese military.

Al-Turabi's movement was established except for the Christian minority in south Sudan. However, Al-Turabi is getting rid of them. Al-Turabi is slaughtering the Christians, cutting off their hands and legs, injecting them with the HIV virus—just as Islam taught him. He is showing the world what Islam will do to Christians if it can.

The Sudanese Christians refuse to convert to Islam. They are also poor and cannot afford to pay for the high taxation of being Christians; therefore, they are dying by the thousands under the authority of al-Turabi. Al-Turabi's Islamic authority has killed Christian men, gathered Christian women and children, and sold them into slavery. Many humanitarian organizations have rushed in to buy these Christian slaves and set them free.

SUMMARY

In summary, though the highly organized fundamentalist group in Egypt did not succeed in overturning its own government, the people who were a part of it went out to influence radical groups in other countries, particularly Libya, Tunisia, Algeria and Sudan.

These movements are gradually becoming a part of our world, and their mission is to take over. They're always waiting for the right environment or a conflict to happen.

Chapter 23

New Strategy: Attack the West

Sheikh Omar Abdel Rahman and Osama bin Laden

THE PRACTICE OF terrorism has evolved since the early seventies in two points—first, the target and second, the method. In the early seventies we started to see a major shift in the targets of terrorism. Terrorists used to target certain individuals such as diplomatic figures, high-ranking military officials and politicians. Today terrorism is no longer threatening individuals, but instead it is focused on the general public.

Random attacks on the public are more effective because they terrorize the majority and spread fear in a larger way. They give terrorists fast results and more bargaining power to get what they want. Terrorism has become a method of political debate and dialogue.

SHEIKH OMAR ABDEL RAHMAN COMES TO AMERICA

After Sheikh Abdel Rahman won his case in front of the Egyptian supreme court, he was given his freedom. He went to Sudan and was welcomed by his fellow jihad leader Dr.

Hasan al-Turabi. Sheikh Abdel Rahman spent a few months there, giving him support.

Then Sheikh Abdel Rahman decided to make a new move toward bringing back the glory of Islam. This time the goal was not to fight any one country—he was pursuing global jihad. Remember, Sayyid Qutb and other writers emphasized the importance of taking jihad to the world and establishing a worldwide Islamic nation.

Sheikh Abdel Rahman was now after what Muslims call the source of infidelity and evil—America and Europe. To work toward this goal, Sheikh Abdel Rahman decided to take advantage of the freedom and democracy that only exist in the West. He came to America.

When Sheikh Abdel Rahman arrived in New Jersey, he received a great welcome from the Muslim leaders of the United States. He settled in New Jersey and immediately started meetings at al-Salaam Mosque in Jersey City. Muslims from all over the United States also invited him to come and teach them. He held seminars and training sessions in many major cities.

What do you think he was teaching them? Love, peace and forgiveness in Islam? Not at all! He taught the American Muslims the true meaning of jihad. He called all American Muslims to unite and work together for the call of Islam, the call for Islam to once again rule the world.

1993 WORLD TRADE CENTER ATTACK

The only goal of Sheikh Abdel Rahman's residency in the United States was to lead jihad from within. The following are his objectives:

- Base the Islamic jihad movement in nations of the

infidels—these are his own words—in preparation
for the worldwide revolution.

● To pressure the U.S. government by threatening
America's security from within.

● To use this pressure to change U.S. policies in the
Islamic world—particularly to break down support
for Israel and to resolve the Palestinian dilemma.

America supports Israel and different governments in the
Middle East that are considered secular by Muslim fundamentalists. Sheikh Abdel Rahman believes these
governments should all be overturned by the sword of Islam.
Therefore, America's support for them makes it the world's
greatest obstacle to the Islamic jihad movement

Sheikh Abdel Rahman's first operation of business was to
shake the United States by attacking one of the foremost sym-
bols of prosperity, success and free enterprise—the towers of
the World Trade Center in New York City. In 1993, as the
world heard, the jihad movement was responsible for a major
explosion in one of the towers, killing six people. For leading
this attack, Sheikh Abdel Rahman will be in a U.S. federal
prison for life. Yes, he's still alive, and we are feeding and pro-
viding for him with taxpayers' money while he continues to
inspire the jihad movement from behind bars.

OBSTACLES TO WORLDWIDE REVOLUTION

The Islamic movement believes there are three main ideolo-
gies that stand in the way of worldwide Islamic revolution.

1. Judaism, as manifested in Israel
2. Christianity, as manifested in the United States
   and the West

3. Communism, as manifested in the former Soviet Union and China

They also believe these obstacles must be destroyed before the revolution will take place.

AMERICA AS A SPECIAL TARGET

There are five clear reasons why America is a special target of Islamic fundamentalists.

1. America represents those whom the Quran calls "People of the Book"—Jews and Christians.

2. America supports Israel.

3. America is the source of all that Muslims consider to be evil—pornography, alcohol, homosexual rights, evil music, evil fashion and evil culture.

4. America supports Christianity all over the world. More Christian missionaries come from the United States than any other country.

5. America is a government "of the people, by the people and for the people," which makes it a heathen government in Muslim thinking because Allah is to be the head of all government.

America and the West are seen as the true enemies of Allah and Islam. The West is always helping Arab governments to kill the Muslim fundamentalists and destroy their organizations. Also, the West helps Israel fight and kill the Arabs.

OSAMA BIN LADEN

There is a new leader in the Islamic movement. He is a Saudi millionaire with a history similar to Sheikh Abdel Rahman's. He left his home country because of persecution from the government and went to Sudan for a short time, just as Abdel Rahman did. In 1996 he left to go to Afghanistan to unite with Dr. Ayman al-Zawahiri and other original members of the Egyptian al-Jihad to establish the al-Qaeda organization. This is an international organization that includes non-Arab members such as Chechnya, Kashmir, Uzbekistan, Pakistan, Kenya and many others. The people are different, but the goal is the same: to declare war on the West, the United States and Israel. Israel is condemned for representing Judaism, and the United States is condemned for representing Christianity.

THE AL-QAEDA ORGANIZATION

Osama bin Laden did not start from nothing. Al-Qaeda is a repackaging, regrouping and reorganization of the Egyptian al-Jihad experience. However, al-Qaeda is different in the following three areas:

Mind-set: Attacking Western targets

Previous Islamic movements believed that they should start locally—overturn their homeland first, establish a nation that is solely based on Islamic authority and then overtake the world. After their failure to take control of Egypt in the eighties, Dr. Zawahiri and Sheikh Abdel Rahman concluded that it would be better to go for worldwide jihad. They decided to go after the "head" rather than the "hands."

The head was identified by its political policies. America and Europe supported Egypt to destroy the Islamic sects; America supported Iraq to fight the fundamentalists of the Iranian revolution; and America is still supporting Israel to fight Palestine. Al-Qaeda decided that America is the head, and the secular Arabic countries are the hands. (Remember, militant fundamentalists consider nearly all Muslim governments to be overly secular.)

Their mind-set is: If we take out the head, then the hands won't work. In other words, if we take out the big brother, then we can do whatever we want to the little brothers.

So the leadership decided the West should be the prime target for al-Qaeda. Bin Laden was convinced of Sheikh Abdel Rahman's new philosophy that jihad, the battle against Islam's enemies, should be fought on the enemy's turf.

Preparation: Diverse, international membership

The target is no longer the police force, the military or the government. Now the target is civilization, economy and the security of the world's source of power, meaning the United States and European countries. The new philosophy for the Islamic movement is one of killing civilians and destroying economies, but it's still in accordance with the Quran.

Because the target has changed, the preparation is different. Al-Qaeda seeks worldwide membership, which gives the group a wide diversity of experience. Osama bin Laden is a multimillionaire, and he used all his wealth to help his movement. He also received a lot of help from the Taliban regime, which confiscated a large selection of weapons from the Russians after their war and also from the U.S., which supported the Afghans' efforts against communism.

Perhaps the most important preparation for al-Qaeda's members is that most of them are experienced soldiers of war. Many of bin Laden's people are survivors of the Egyptian jihad movement, the Afghanistan war, the Kashmir war, the war against Israel and many other conflicts. These men are trained terrorists, rejected by their own governments.

Implementation: Starting with smaller targets

Implementation of the plan started by learning from Sheikh Abdel Rahman's example. He failed in the first bomb attack against the World Trade Center in 1993. Al-Qaeda learned from past mistakes and made better plans: They began with smaller U.S. targets. On August 7, 1998, they bombed the U.S. embassies in both Kenya and Tanzania, killing more than two hundred people. The U.S. response was weak: On August 20, 1998, President Bill Clinton launched two cruise missiles against suspected terrorist sites in Sudan. Al-Qaeda laughed at the Clinton administration for using multimillion-dollar missiles to blow up ten-dollar tents.

Later, on October 12, 2000, al-Qaeda tried to sink one of America's largest Navy ships, the *USS Cole*, as it sat in the harbor at Aden, Yemen. The bomb killed seventeen sailors, injured many others and sent America's great ship home with a huge hole in the middle. This time the administration did not retaliate. It acted as if nothing happened. Now al-Qaeda perceived a message of tolerance from the United States, and bin Laden got the green light to do bigger and worse—attacking on U.S. soil for the first time since the 1993 bombing of the World Trade Center. On September 11, 2001, his plan was put into action as four planes were hijacked. This act resulted in the collapse of the World Trade Center and damage to the Pentagon—not to mention the deaths of everyone on board the planes.

The worldwide media was instrumental in helping al-Qaeda achieve its goal of spreading fear and shaking the West's national security, especially that of the United States.

Sayyid Qutb envisioned this in his writings—Muslims moving the battleground to the infidel's homeland and ruling the world by the fear of Islam. This is what Sheikh Abdel Rahman started, and now Osama bin Laden is continuing.

Osama bin Laden learned a lot from the experience of Egyptians in al-Qaeda, especially his right-hand man, Ayman al-Zawahiri, and others. You can see a lot of similarity between the technique used by the Egyptian al-Jihad in their attempt to take over the government and al-Qaeda's methods against the U.S. The Egyptian al-Jihad stole from Christians and used an Egyptian soldier trained by the government to use a military weapon to assassinate President Sadat. Al-Qaeda stole from the U.S. (four aircraft) and used them to attack its targets.

The innocent Christians in cities all over Egypt (Nagh Hamadi, Abo Karacas, Al Minya, Dyroot, Malawi, Asyut, and others) were the cheap sacrifice for the Islamic terrorists' game, as were the Americans in New York, Washington, D.C., and the planes' passengers and flight crews.

Killing innocent people in the name of Allah is a continual practice of Islam worldwide. It is going on with millions of Christians in the south Sudan, Egypt, Nigeria and other countries.

A good example is what happened in January 2000 in Al-Kosheh, a village in southern Egypt. Twenty-one men, women and children were set on fire with torches and burned to death during an attack on their village. Their bodies were split open vertically from the throat down so their attackers could watch their organs pulsate; others were set on fire while still alive. The perpetrators cut opposite arms and legs off to send back to their village to spread fear.[1]

Where do militant Muslims get the ideas for their cruelty? From the Quran.

> The recompense of those who wage war against Allah
> and His Messenger and do mischief in the land is only
> that they shall be killed or crucified or their hands and
> their feet be cut off from opposite sides, or be exiled
> from the land.
>
> —SURAH 5:33, *THE NOBLE QURAN*

While this English translation says to cut off hands and feet, my understanding of the Arabic meaning is to cut off the entire arm and leg, just as they did to the Egyptian villagers.

Yes, this is happening in the twenty-first century. Of course, the Egyptian government did a good job of covering up what happened.

SECTION V

MUSLIMS AND THE GOOD NEWS

The False Christianity Presented to Muslims

Silent Christians, Mixed-up Trinity, Closed Church Doors

IWAS BORN AND raised in Egypt, the heart of the Islamic and Arabic world. All my years in Egypt I heard about Christianity from two sources—first, from Al-Azhar where I studied Islam and other religions, and second, from my family, my neighbors, society and the Egyptian media.

Both sources were presenting a false Christianity, not the true Christianity that I have discovered since I met the Lord Jesus Christ. They were not interested in presenting Christianity as Christians know and believe. They presented Christianity as it was described by the Quranic verses and Islamic teaching.

At the same time, Egypt was and is home to a very large Christian denomination, which has millions of members in its congregations. This church has thousands of branches in different cities and villages in Egypt. This one large group makes up about 95 percent of the Christians in Egypt. The other 5 percent is comprised of a variety of Protestant denominations.

I could see Christians wherever I went in my country. They lived in my neighborhood, worked in the businesses and supermarkets, even in government buildings. However, not even one Christian person tried to talk to me about his Jesus Christ and his own Christian faith except the wonderful pharmacist who gave me the Bible to read. (She suffered some persecution for that act. Fundamentalists tried to burn down her pharmacy, and she ultimately left Egypt and went to Canada.)

Christians living in Egypt are a minority. They have been and still are persecuted by the Muslim fundamentalist groups. So they have decided to live quietly and to distance themselves as much as possible from the more than 50 million Muslims living in the country who need to hear about Jesus Christ. This Christian society lives under great fear, and they actually refuse to witness to Muslims.

MY CHRISTIAN ROOMMATE

After I earned my bachelor's degree, I was required to spend one year in the Egyptian military. I shared a room with one other solider, who happened to be a Christian. I knew he was a Christian because our government identification cards list whether you are Christian or Muslim. He had a business degree.

During this time, I questioned him constantly about his faith. "How can you believe in three gods?" I asked, referring to the Trinity. "You are an educated man. How can you believe something so stupid?" I asked him how he could believe that God has a son. "Does God have a wife?" I mocked. All these concepts were blasphemous according to Islam.

Whenever I questioned him, he refused to answer. He would say to me, "Let us just be friends. Leave religion to

God, please. Don't question me about religion, my faith or your faith." He was very fearful of me and of the Muslims in our military group. Though he was never physically hurt, I think this was one of the most difficult years of his life.

After I met the Lord Jesus Christ, I remembered this man. I was very sorry for how he allowed the spirit of fear to control his life and how he refused to share the true Jesus Christ with others. If this man had been willing to allow the Lord to use him in my life or in another person's life in our military group, he could have accomplished a great thing and brought about the salvation of many Muslims.

THE CHURCH DOORS CLOSED TO ME

I remember with great sadness how the Egyptian church had little interest in reaching out to Muslims. When I went back to the Christian pharmacist who had given me the Bible and declared my faith in Jesus Christ in front of her, she arranged to go with me to meet the leader of an Egyptian church. She hoped this man would adopt me spiritually and baptize me. She also hoped that he would help me in biblical study and receive me as a new member of the body of Jesus Christ.

We sat down together in his office, and he basically told me, "My son, you can go back to your home. We do not need to add a number to our congregation. And if you go home, we will not lose any number from our congregation. We are not interested."

As we were leaving his office I told him, "Listen, you need help. I am not worried about what you did to me now. The One who saved me will help me and will look after me. Even though you reject me, He will be faithful to me wherever I go."

On my way back from the church to home, I tried hard to understand what this Christian leader did. I expected him to be excited and happy to hear my story because it was proof that God was working in the lives of Muslim peoples. I thought he would be like Jesus' disciples in the Bible, who were known by their love for others.

But I also remembered a Christian monk from my childhood. I attacked a donkey he was riding on and caused him to have a serious head injury, but he showed great mercy to me afterwards. I decided there was just something wrong with this one priest.

Later the priest explained to my pharmacist friend that he didn't want other Muslims to hear that he had opened up his church to a Muslim because he was afraid they would come and burn down the building.

This church leader had decided to live in peace and quietness by shutting the door and dealing only with his congregation. Some Christians in Egypt have the attitude that "We were born Christians, so we are Christians. You were born Muslim, so you are a Muslim." They have no idea that a Muslim can be saved and become a Christian.

There are churches that evangelize in Egypt, but they are very, very few—about 5 percent. They represent a variety of Protestant denominations, including Assemblies of God, Anglican and others. They try to witness in secret to Muslims.

After years of growing in my faith in Christ, I sometimes think about that meeting with the priest. I spoke the truth when I said, "You need help," because he *did* need help to understand his destiny in Jesus Christ. A Christian leader or person serving the Lord cannot allow the spirit of fear to control his life and force him to adopt a callous attitude toward new Christians. The attitude of this priest, which is common in the Middle East, is another part of the false Christianity that is presented to Muslims.

QURAN PRESENTS FALSE CHRISTIANITY

Islam presents Christianity to Muslims through the Quranic verses as a religion created by men, not Jesus Himself. For example, they say Paul was the founder of Christianity, not Jesus. They claim Jesus never said He was God and should be worshiped.

> And (remember) when Allah will say (on the Day of Resurrection): "O Isa (Jesus), son of Maryam (Mary)! Did you say unto men: 'Worship me and my mother as two gods besides Allah?'" He [Jesus] will say: "Glory be to you [Allah]! It was not for me to say what I had no right (to say)... Never did I say to them aught except what You (Allah) did command me to say: 'Worship Allah, my Lord and your Lord.'"
>
> —SURAH 5:116–117, *THE NOBLE QURAN*

Even Sayyid Qutb espoused this view in his Quranic commentary, *In the Shadows of the Quran.*

There is also a great misunderstanding among Muslims regarding the Trinity. They believe Christians are worshiping three gods—but not Father, Son and Holy Spirit. They see it as God the Father, Jesus the Son and Mary the mother of God. The idea that God has a mother is absolutely ridiculous to them.

There are two sources for this thinking.

1. *The traditional Christian churches in the Middle East give a lot of attention to Mary.* They have icons and pictures of Mary in the church, and they kneel or bow in front of them. Muslims see this as idol worship. Christian people will pray, "Mary, mother of God, ask your Son to forgive our sins."

If you asked one of these Christians, "Do you worship Mary and believe she is God?" he will reply, "No. We just adore and respect her as the mother of God." (Remember, when the Muslim hears "mother of God" he is completely turned off.) In Egypt, Christian leaders claim to see apparitions of Mary weeping for the persecution of the church. Even a former leader of this denomination claimed he saw an apparition of Mary on the top of a monastery in Egypt.

2. *The Quran refers to the worship of Mary.* In the quotation from the Quran above, you see a reference to worshiping Mary as god besides Allah. Even in Muhammad's day, the Christians of Arabia had statues and icons of Mary. They venerated her to the extent that Muhammad perceived the church to be worshiping her, and thus Muhammad received Quranic verses on this issue.

In all the confusion, the Holy Spirit became equated with the angel Gabriel. So when Muhammad received revelations from an angel that called itself Gabriel, he thought that Gabriel was the Holy Spirit.

Another issue is the Muslims' perception that Christians must go through other human beings to get to God. Muslims believe that they pray directly to Allah. Not even Muhammad can come between them and Allah. Five times a day their prayers go directly to Allah. Therefore they have a very negative reaction to the position of the priest in the traditional church. Muslims will not accept any person as a mediator between man and God. They won't accept the idea that they must confess to the priest so that their sins will be forgiven.

The traditional church in the Middle East seems to have many gods, from the Muslim point of view, in the form of saints. The church believes the saints have the power to show themselves to Christians and the power to do miracles in their lives, even though they died hundreds of years ago. For example, my Christian roommate in the military carried a picture of one of the former popes of the church. I asked him one day, "Why do you carry that picture? Who is this man?"

He said, "This is one of the past popes of our church. I carry his picture wherever I go because he is my protector; he's the one who hears my cry when I am in trouble."

It was only after I was saved and studied the Word of God for myself that I got a right understanding of the concept of the Trinity and that I understood there is no person—dead or alive—who can be my protector except my Savior and my Lord.

Muslims need grace from God to understand the Trinity and the Christian faith. It would help tremendously if the church in the Middle East presented a clearer picture about Jesus Christ and His message of salvation. Jesus is the only one to mediate between man and God. They do not need a person to come in the picture and make the confusion worse.

Bringing the Gospel to Muslims

Ten Commandments to Follow

A FTER MY FATHER pulled a gun on me, I fled my native country. The Lord Jesus told me to go to South Africa. There He sent true brothers and sisters to help me have the victory of Jesus Christ over the old Muslim man in me. They decided to send me to a six-month discipleship school with a group called Youth With A Mission. There I received the victory, and I started to experience the new man in Jesus Christ inside me.

When I had been established in Christian faith, I began to share the good news with my Muslim brothers. In Durban, South Africa, the Lord led me to an Egyptian Muslim. He came to the Lord, and within one week his Muslim wife from India also accepted Jesus Christ.

For one month he translated for me as I worked among the English-speaking Muslims of South Africa. Seven Muslims converted, which was a great victory. The news of this reached a Lebanese missionary who said he had been praying for four years for a Muslim convert to come help his organization reach Muslims in South Africa. It was through this missionary that I spoke for the first time in a church. I spoke in Arabic, and this missionary translated for me.

I had a lot of opportunities to speak at churches. However, at the same time we wanted to continue to reach out to the Muslim communities. To do this, we arranged a debate between a well-known Muslim leader in Johannesburg named Abdul-Kadir and myself. We met at the Statesman Hotel, and about two hundred fifty Muslims came. It was during the holy month of Ramadan, which put religious fervor at a high pitch.

As we were finishing, I heard a man shouting. A Muslim man ran into the meeting room waving a large knife and screaming, "Where is the Egyptian dog? Where is the Egyptian infidel? I will kill him and drink his blood this evening." He had obviously been drinking alcohol (which is really against Islamic law). He ran through the crowd and came at me with the knife. The missionary got between us and was trying to get the knife out of his hand.

Then eight African men from the crowd came at us. I was afraid that they were on this man's side. But instead they grabbed him and took his knife away. Then they began to hit him with their fists and kick him. Finally, they picked him up and threw him out of the hotel.

When they came back in the meeting room they addressed the Muslim leader that I had debated and told him, "We are converting from Islam, and we accept Jesus Christ. God saved this man, and he is serving the true God."

At this point, the crowd was in a frenzy. These eight men surrounded us to keep the people back. Several of them picked me up and carried me on their shoulders as we ran out of the hotel. The missionary ran alongside us. We made it to the missionary's car, and these men surrounded the car until he got the door open, we climbed inside, and we drove away.

The eight who came to Christ that day escaped the crowd unharmed. They were Muslims from Algeria who had come to South Africa looking for work. The missionary and I discipled them, meeting with them on a weekly basis. We helped several of them go to Bible school, and one of the Bible school graduates is ministering to Muslim children in Pretoria.

Several days after this debate, I was walking to the supermarket to buy groceries when two men stopped me on the street and attacked me with knives. I was cut on the top of the head and was taken to Alberton Clinic Hospital, where I spent three days recovering. The men were also from Algeria, and it was obvious retaliation for the conversions that had occurred.

The South African media started to report on the persecution I was facing. This media coverage opened the door for me to share my testimony in churches all over the country.

I have spoken more than two thousand times in the last eight years. This includes places all over the world, but especially in South Africa, where I lived until 1999.

Setting Captives Free

Since I came to Jesus Christ, my heart has not stopped crying out for the Muslims who are in bondage to Islam. We must set them free with the gospel. I hope that you, dear reader, are one of those who will play a role in this mission.

We love the Muslim people with the love of God. We oppose Islam, which keeps them in bondage, but we love the people. And we must have the courage to reach out and touch their need with the gospel of love.

Islam is the world's second largest religion with 1.3 billion followers. More than one-fifth of humankind follows Islam. It is the world's fastest-growing religion, due to high birthrates and conversions.[1] At the same time, remember that Christianity is the world's largest religion (2 billion followers). That should give confidence that the Muslim world can be reached with the gospel.

God will not allow Islam to continue to mislead the Muslim nations and cause them to stray from Him eternally. God is "not willing that any should perish, but that all should come to repentance" (2 Pet. 3:9, KJV).

Muslims are hungry for truth because they are disenchanted with the spirit of deception in Islam. Muslims are thirsty for love, forgiveness and mercy. Muslims are searching for peace in this world because they are disillusioned by the religious jihad, which leads to bloodshed and hatred. Women are frustrated with persecution and denial of their rights. Muslims are longing for a personal relationship with God as their Savior.

I have been reaching out to Muslims for many years, and there are some things you should be aware of when you reach out to them.

TEN COMMANDMENTS FOR SHARING THE GOSPEL WITH MUSLIMS

1. Use the Word of God.

Muslims respect the sacred books: the Law of Moses, the Book of Psalms, the Gospels and the Quran. Let the Word of God speak for itself. The Gospels are the best portions to start with, particularly Matthew and Luke.

2. Be constantly in prayer.

It is the Holy Spirit who wins men to Christ. Seek His

guidance and power as you present the Word.

3. Be a genuine friend.

Saying "Hello. How are you?" isn't enough. If you really care, show it by inviting them to your home, sharing your time and helping with their problems.

4. Ask thought-provoking questions.

Help them to reach their own conclusions about the gospel. Good questions to ask are:

- Do you have assurance that God will accept you?

- What does the Quran teach about forgiveness?

- May I show you what the Bible teaches?

Questions like these show that you have an interest in the important things of life.

5. Listen attentively.

When you ask a question, courtesy requires that you listen to the answer no matter how long it takes. You'll be surprised at how much you'll learn.

6. Present your beliefs openly.

State what you believe, clearly and without apology, showing Scripture passages that support those teachings. Thus, you place the responsibility for doctrine where it belongs—on the Word of God.

Talk about sin and how it affects our lives. Say, "Sin is the biggest problem in our world today. How do we deal with sin?" A person who is living in sin hates himself. He is an enemy to himself. Most Muslims recognize that they are living in sin, but they don't know how to get forgiveness. Tell them how Jesus forgives sins.

7. Reason, don't argue.

Argument may win a point but lose a hearing. There are some points on which you can argue forever without achieving a thing, except closing a mind against you.

8. Never denigrate Muhammad or the Quran.

This is as offensive to them as speaking disrespectfully about Christ or the Bible is to us.

9. Respect their customs and sensitivities.

Don't offend by:

- Putting your Bible (a holy book) on the floor.

- Speaking too freely about sex. (Muslims don't speak about sex; it is considered dirty.)

- Appearing too familiar in casual relationships with the opposite sex.

- Refusing hospitality.

- Making jokes about sacred topics such as fasting, prayer or God.

- Offering them pork or alcohol.

Women would be more acceptable to practicing Muslims if they wore a long dress as opposed to pants or shorts.

10. Persevere.

Muslims have a lot of rethinking to do when they are confronted with the gospel, but rest assured that the Word of God will do its work in His good time.

Above all, be humble. Speak with love. This will make a way for you. My cries and my prayers to the Lord Jesus Christ are to draw millions of Muslims to His kingdom.

THE CONFESSION OF FAITH

When a Muslim is interested in praying to accept Jesus as Lord and Savior, I always verify that he understands the step he is about to take. I ask, "Do you believe in Jesus Christ and the Bible, and that Jesus died on the cross for the forgiveness of your sins?" Then I continue, "Where does Muhammad stand as the prophet of Islam? Where do you stand with your Islamic faith?"

Many times the person will reply, "In the past I knew Jesus as one of the prophets of God who brought Christianity to the world. Now I understand that He really is the Son of God, that He died on the cross and that my sins are going to be forgiven by His blood. But I also believe Muhammad is one of the prophets of God and that the Quran is from God."

I have to say, "No, friend, Muhammad and Jesus Christ cannot meet together. The Quran and the Bible cannot stand together." Then I explain what Muhammad did not do for the Muslim and what Jesus Christ can do for him. I take him through a short comparison between how his life is with Muhammad and how his life would be with Jesus.

At this point I confirm where this Muslim person is standing. I make sure he denies Muhammad as the prophet of God and the Quran as the Word of God. The person must also promise to cut off any relationship with Islamic faith. After this I lead him in prayer for salvation.

You cannot end your relationship with this person after the prayer. This is the beginning of a very important time of discipleship. Without extra attention, the new Muslim convert is very likely to be drawn back to Islam. The next chapter will tell you how you can help these new converts.

Chapter 26

Challenges for Muslim Converts

Special Ways to Help Muslim Converts

L ET ME TELL you a story to illustrate how a Muslim can be hungry for the gospel just as I was.

One time I had traveled to Cape Town, South Africa, to speak for a missionary and his wife. The man had picked me up in his car, and we went to pick up his wife at a Muslim lady's house. When we arrived, this man's wife told the Muslim lady that a professor from Al-Azhar was in the car. This Muslim lady became very excited and wanted us to come in and have a cup of tea, so we agreed.

When we entered this house, I could see that she was poor and there was almost nothing in the house. As we talked, this lady realized I was no longer Muslim, and she became very upset with me. "How can you betray Islam?" she complained.

I told her, "I am very tired now, but I will tell you two stories." These are the stories I told her.

> One time a woman was brought to Muhammad who had committed adultery. They asked him, "What shall

we do with her?" Muhammad said, "Go away. Bring
her back after the baby is born."

So they brought her back after the baby was born,
and Muhammad said, "Let her go and nurse the child.
Bring her back when the child is two years old."

So they brought her back, and Muhammad said,
"Take the baby from her and kill her." And that is what
they did.

Now let us compare Muhammad to Jesus. There
was a time when people brought a woman to Jesus who
had been caught in adultery. "Shall we stone her?" the
people said. Jesus replied, "Let him who is without sin
cast the first stone." Everybody went away. There was
no one left to stone her because they all knew they had
sinned. Then Jesus said, "Neither do I condemn you.
Go and sin no more."

I ask you, whom do you want to follow—
Muhammad or Jesus?

The woman burst out in tears and cried out, "I am that
woman." She had been in an adulterous relationship and was
now pregnant. When her Muslim family found out that she
was pregnant, they tried to kill her. She ran away, and some
of her friends helped her to rent this little house.

She accepted Jesus that day, and my friends took her to
their house for three days to explain the Christian faith to
her. They continued to disciple her after that as well.

SPECIAL CHALLENGES

You can see how the Lord will prepare the Muslim's heart to
hear the gospel. But remember that a person who comes to
Christ out of Islam is different from someone who had no
faith and then accepts Jesus.

Even though the Muslim convert is a baby Christian, he or she was a full-grown Muslim before coming to Christ. There is already a strong religious belief system in place. So the convert will face special challenges in his or her walk with Christ. This happened in my life also.

The issues that need to be dealt with probably won't be ones of sexual morality or drinking alcohol, because those things were already prescribed in Islam. The issues are more matters of the heart—a judgmental attitude, a misunderstanding about the true nature of God.

After learning to grow in Christ myself, as well as discipling many Muslim converts, I have noticed some issues that almost always need to be addressed. These are:

Salvation through Christ

Be sure to teach them that there is no salvation without believing that Jesus Christ is the Son of God and fully God.

Forgiveness for sins

Under Islam, Muslims can pray to Allah for forgiveness, but they cannot know whether their sins are forgiven or not. Be sure to teach the new believer that all sins are forgiven after accepting the Lord Jesus Christ. This is something a new believer really needs to understand from God's Word because he or she will tend to doubt God's forgiveness.

Discipleship

In order to have victory over the old Muslim man, the new believer needs to be living in fellowship with the body of Christ. The body of Christ must help him to settle into a church (it would be helpful if the church were close to his house). Someone from the church needs to accept responsibility for this person to grow in Christ. The new convert must be accountable to this person on a weekly or daily basis. This must be a relationship where the new convert can ask questions and talk through problems.

Bible reading—especially Acts and Romans

Reading the Bible every day is very important. In the beginning, I especially recommend the Book of Acts and the Book of Romans.

The Book of Acts shows the Muslim that true faith is not spread by the sword, as it is in Islam. Islam is spread by people killing in the name of Allah, but Christianity does not rule by force. In the Book of Acts Jesus' disciples spread the Good News without a military army, a sword or force—just by the Spirit of God and the Word of God. The new believer will learn that he or she does not have to think about killing in the name of Christ. Instead, his calling is to live by the Spirit of God and the Word of God and to present the love and peace of God to the world around him.

The Book of Romans is an important book because it deals deeply with sin. The Muslim old man is still a big influence on the new believer. To overcome this he must read and understand Romans—seeing the struggle between spirit and flesh.

A former Muslim has no idea about walking with the Spirit because all his life he has been living by the flesh. He or she must overcome the influence of the Islamic law. Show him how to live by the righteousness of God.

Bible study

The new convert must get involved in serious Bible study. It is good for him to study alone or in a cell group, but it is also necessary to have more intense study in a Bible study group or with an individual. It can be as simple as reading a chapter of Scripture together and discussing what it means. Be sure to ask the new believer's opinion about what you read. It shouldn't be a one-sided conversation. This type of Bible study will also help the mentor see how the person is growing in Christ.

Intense Bible study will probably cause the new convert to ask some questions that compare the Bible to the Quran. This is because the Quran contains references to biblical teaching, but with significant differences. It is good to let the person bring these questions to you and answer them together. It is *not* a good idea to systematically go through the Quran and show where it is wrong. Focus on what the Bible says instead.

In addition, the mentor can provide the new believer with good books, tapes and Christian magazines.

The new prayer life

The new believer needs help from the body of Christ to see the difference between prayer in Islam and prayer in Christ. Prayer in Islam is prayer by the law. Muslims must pray five times a day, not four times or three times. When they pray, they repeat the same words and actions every time. It is just an automatic ritual.

Christian prayer is not dictated by a law. It is a relationship between the believer and Christ. The new believer may think that Christians only pray on Sunday in church, so he needs to understand that a Christian makes time to pray every day. This time is when you sit with your Father, share what is going on inside of you and ask Him to guide you.

Under Islam, a person must do a ritual cleaning before going to prayer. This involves using water on the arms, hands, ear, nose, face, hair and feet. If water is not available, then clean dust from the ground is used. After accepting Jesus, the Muslim is cleansed by Jesus' blood. Let him know he can go to God in prayer just as he is because he has been washed by the blood of Jesus.

Follow Jesus, not other Christians

The difference of opinions between Christians confuses a new Muslim believer. His source for knowing how to live the Christian life must be Jesus, not other Christians. He must use the Word to decide whether or not he is doing the right things. He must become skilled at using the Word of God to decide what action to take. Just as he lived by the Quran as a Muslim, he must live by the Word of God as a Christian. Some people will say they are Christians but not behave in a Christlike way. God will never disappoint a convert, but Christians can. The problem is in the heart of man.

Racial prejudice

A Muslim knows a lot about prejudice from a religious point of view. In Islam, you are prejudiced against people of every other religion. But Muslims have not known prejudice against the color of their skin. It should never happen in church, but if it does, it can be devastating. The new believer will be quick to reject church for any discrimination. Former Muslims will not let anyone in the world look down on them because of their skin color.

When I was a young Christian in South Africa, I had some white Christians walk out of a church service because I was the speaker. Afterward, when I learned why they had left, it was like a bomb going off in my brain. It was the first time I was ever looked down on because of my color. I went to my home questioning God, "How can these people be Christian? I was accepted by You. How could they reject me?" I had to go to the Word of God to teach me, "There is neither Jew nor Greek, slave nor free, male nor female, for you are all one in Christ Jesus" (Gal. 3:28). Man disappoints; God will not.

(You may be surprised to know that moderate Muslims do not look down on Caucasians. They actually respect them for their accomplishments in technology, education and so on. Only fanatic Muslims condemn whites for their skin color.)

Discussing doubts

As soon as a Muslim accepts Jesus, Satan comes to try to make him doubt Jesus, the Word of God, church and so forth. The new believer must know that he can take any doubts or questions to his mentor or the leader of the church. They can help him get over the obstacle through showing him the answer in the Word of God, offering him counsel and praying with him.

Westerners may be surprised at some of the issues that offer great challenges for former Muslims. For example, I met with a former Muslim lady at a church in the United States. She was baptized and a member of the church, but she was struggling with some issues. It came from the strict teaching in Islam regarding sexual purity. To explain briefly, sexual relationship is treated like something dirty in Islamic teaching. After a sexual relationship, a Muslim must do a complete washing that includes immersing the entire body in water. This must be done before he can go to prayer, enter a mosque or even touch the Quran. Muslims experience tremendous guilt if they break this law. In addition, the sexes are kept separate as much as possible. Even in the mosque, the men sit in the front and the women and children sit in the back or high in a balcony where they can't be seen.

So this Christian woman was very bothered by something she saw during the church service. A boy and girl were sitting next to each other with their arms around each other. The boy was playing with the girl's hair during the sermon. This former Muslim couldn't believe their lack of respect for the house of God.

I told her how I too struggled with these kinds of issues when I first became a Christian. Then I explained, "Christians are free people. They are set free by the blood of Jesus. No culture or rules control their lives. They must live by righteousness and faith in God. The actions of this young man do not turn the church into a nightclub. The important thing is the relationship between the Christian and his God. If the young man is a true believer and living with God, he will not do anything immoral with this girl."

Freedom in Christ

Muslims are not used to the freedom Christians have. The rules of Christianity deal with the heart, while the laws of Islam deal with what is done on the outside. So a new convert from Islam can be offended and judgmental when another person's outward appearance does not seem to be proper based on the new believer's past experience. For example, when I was a student with Youth With A Mission in South Africa, our class met with another class for a lecture. I noticed that a young man from the other class had long hair. This really confused me. *God*, I thought, *is this a man or a woman?*

During a break I went to my leader and said, "Why does he have long hair? He is like a woman." (I think this was really a cultural issue for me from my Egyptian heritage.) The leader opened my Bible to Luke 7:3, which says, "Why do you look

at the speck of sawdust in your brother's eye and pay no attention to the plank in your own eye?" He counseled me, "Go to
this brother and tell him what we talked about. Ask him to
forgive you." That is what I did, and the young man received
me in the love of God. This is how I grew as a baby Christian.

Facing problems

A new believer must learn that even though he is a
Christian he will face problems. Problems are a test of faith
and trust in Christ. Don't let problems take him away from
Christ. Present the Word: "And we know that in all things
God works for the good of those who love him, who have
been called according to his purpose" (Rom. 8:28). Point out
that other Christians are also dealing with problems.

Addressing financial needs

It is a very good idea for the church to find out about the
financial needs of a new believer—if he or she needs help getting a job or paying bills. This is because of what he saw at the
mosque. In Egypt, for example, if a Christian converts to
Islam, the mosque will give him money, help them find a job
and so forth. The same would occur at a mosque in the United
States. If a single mom with children were to convert to Islam,
the mosque would take good care of her—provide childcare,
provide money, pay her rent and help her find work. They
would not leave her alone. Muslims in the mosque who have
financial needs may also be helped, but there is special consid-
eration for new converts. So if a new believer is in need and
the church does not help, he will feel rejected.

Attention from the pastor

A Muslim convert is usually suffering from losing family,
home and Muslim society. He needs to feel that he has a new

home at the church. He has been rejected by many who are close to him, so he needs extra love and attention. Attention is just the love of Jesus Christ for this person. When the leader of the church gets involved, it shows the new believer that he or she has truly been accepted.

Getting involved

Let the new believer know everybody in Christ loves him because he has been delivered from darkness and has become a child of the Most High God. But even if everybody in the church feels wonderful about the new believer, it doesn't do any good unless that is expressed to him directly. Without extra confirmation, he may feel left out and discriminated against. It helps to get him involved in church activities.

Avoid Muslim influences

For two to three years, the new believer will be vulnerable to influences from the Muslim life that was left behind. If he or she remains immersed in Muslim society, people will try to make the new believer change his mind and return to Islam. If the new believer has a lot of struggle with fitting into a church and Christian society, it just may seem easier to go back to Islam. The church needs to be the alternative to Muslim society. After the believer is firmly grounded in faith, then he or she can go back and share the gospel with other Muslims.

CONCLUSION

Dear reader, I would like to challenge you to have the courage and the heart of Jesus Christ toward Muslims.

If Jesus Christ were living with us today, He would travel to the Muslim countries. He would enter the mosques and preach the Word of God and the message of salvation just as He did in the temple two thousand years ago.

He would visit Muslim people in their houses or meet with them at the workplace. He would heal Muslims who are sick. He would open the blind Muslims' eyes.

He would declare the forgiveness of God to the Muslim sinners. He would confront Muslims with the truth, and He would tell them about the secret of heaven with love, compassion and care.

He would not forget them. He would not be afraid of them. He would not think that some of them are terrorists and might kill Him or cause Him harm.

Jesus Christ would show the Muslims the way to heaven through Himself, not through Mary, not through saints. The Lord Jesus Christ would never turn Muslims away.

This is my challenge to the church: Open your arms to Muslims. Show them the love of Christ. Tell them that Jesus died for them. Give them the hope that their sins will be forgiven.

When they come to the Lord, encourage them. Help them to be united with the body of Christ.

I praise God for the way He uses His people in the Western church to offer themselves as living sacrifices to work among Muslims even in dangerous conditions. I praise God for the two American girls who were arrested in Afghanistan. Their experience in prison was the Book of Acts brought to life.

Finally, my heart is crying before the Lord for the church in the Middle East to be touched by God's Spirit and to open the door for Muslims to come to the knowledge of Christ.

Epilogue

Prince of Peace

EAR READER, I believe you may be feeling shocked after reading this book. When you read about some of the things done in the name of Islam, it is hard to believe that human beings could commit such acts against other human beings. However, these are the facts. I speak from personal experience.

What motivates these people? From my own experience I can say that Muslim secret police did not kidnap and torture me because they hated me personally. Nor did my father try to kill me because he never loved me. The men on the street did not try to stab me because I had harmed them in any way. All these people believed that I had betrayed Islam, and they were obligated according to the Quran to kill me.

The blame is not on my father or any of the others. The blame lies upon the teaching of the Quran and the prophet of Islam.

They call me an infidel, but I am happy to be an infidel because now I know Jesus. I have experienced Him, and I am worshiping Him and believing the true God. I enjoy my Christian life today and my relationship with God. I never experienced that peace and satisfaction in Islam. The goal of the rest of my life is to continue living with Jesus Christ, to serve Him and to do what I can to take Him to my own people whom I left behind.

I believe that to reach God's children, the Muslims, Christians need to understand the Muslim point of view. That is why you discovered in this book:

- The core beliefs of Islam. In particular, you learned that later revelations cancel out earlier revelations. So the 114 verses in the Quran about peace and patience are canceled by the call to jihad.

- The clear picture about the meaning of jihad in Islam and the development of the practice of jihad by Muslims during the last fourteen hundred years. Jihad activity has victimized the entire world through hatred, killing and bloodshed.

- How the world has been deceived by Muslim mission activity and sometimes by the world media.

- How Egypt has served as the launch pad for Islamic terrorism philosophy and leaders around the world. Influential leaders have included Sheikh Omar Abdel Rahman, Ayman al-Zawahiri, Sayyid Qutb and others. Before this book, it was difficult to see the role of Egypt in Islamic worldwide terrorist activity.

- The most recent development of jihad—taking it to the West—as acted out by Sheikh Abdel Rahman and Osama bin Laden.

Today we are facing a most dangerous enemy to mankind. We are not facing local thugs who seek money or power. We are facing an enemy that is motivated by faith and belief.

They are all reading the same playbook—the Quran. They want nothing less than to control the world and submit it to Islam. They want Islamic authority to be the only form of government in the world.

I do believe the responsibility of every person in the world is to speak out against this type of terrorism—especially the body of Christ. Christians have the responsibility to do spiritual warfare through fasting and prayer, asking the Lord to break down the stronghold of Islam.

Political and military actions have a role to play, but they will not take this evil away. There is only One to rescue us: He is the source of peace and the prince of peace, the Lord Jesus Christ.

The world right now faces two great challenges.

1. *The most horrible relationship you can imagine between Arab Muslims and Jews.* This animosity is not just from Arabic culture. It comes from the Quran. If you read what the Quran says about the Jews, whom it refers to as the children of pigs and monkeys, you would recognize the source of the hatred in the heart of Muslim Arabs. Yasser Arafat, who is a secular Arab Muslim, has an impossible job of pursuing peace with Israel because Hamas and al-Jihad in Palestine have declared jihad against the Jews.

2. *Widespread Islamic terrorism, which started and developed in the Middle East and has now infected the entire world.*

Based on my experience, I believe the cause of these two challenges is that the Christian church in the Middle East failed to present the true Jesus Christ to both Jews and Muslims.

No one can heal the heart of Muslims and set them free except Jesus. When Muslims meet with Jesus and receive His gift of forgiveness and eternal life, they are not going to need to commit suicide or kill others or to die in the name of Allah so that they can avoid hell and go to Paradise.

No political or military power can bring reconciliation between Muslim Arabs and Jews except the blood of Jesus Christ.

When I was in Cape Town, South Africa, I met a Christian Jewish lady named Elizabeth. She invited me to speak in a prayer meeting in her house. When it was my time to share, I asked the people gathered there, "Do you know the most recent miracle Jesus Christ performed?"

They replied, "No."

I said, "Through the blood of Jesus a former Muslim man and a Jewish lady have come together tonight as brothers and sisters in Jesus Christ."

No other power in this world can bring reconciliation between Jews and Arabs.

I encourage every believer in every part of the world to stand up and pray for Muslims and Jews; pray for the light of Jesus Christ to shine on them. The battle is not ours; it's God's. But we are the children of God. We have to stand in the gap. Be sensitive to what the Spirit of God tells you to do to. Sooner or later, the evil of terrorism will be defeated. The stronghold of Islam will fall down, in the name of Jesus.

We will rejoice one day in heaven when we meet with our converted Muslim brothers. We rejoice even today on earth when we see Muslims come to the Lord and become a part of the body of Jesus Christ.

After the horrible act on September 11, 2001, I was stunned by the loss of life. At the same time, I had peace because the Word of God says, "In all things God works for the good of those who love him, who have been called according to his purpose" (Rom. 8:28). The Spirit of the Lord showed me He is going to cause this evil act to expose Islam worldwide, to open the door for millions of people to discover the truth and to lead many of them to the knowledge of our Savior, Jesus Christ.

Notes

CHAPTER 1: DISILLUSIONED AT AL-AZHAR

1. From the hadith recorded by Sahih Al-Bukhari.

CHAPTER 4: CORE BELIEFS OF ISLAM

1. Akbar S. Ahmed, *Islam Today* (London: I.B. Tauris & Co., 1999), pp. 32–38.
2. Several sources confirm the idea that the verse of the sword had replaced and overridden (*nasikh*) the 114 Quranic verses about forgiving the infidels and no longer killing them. These sources include JaLal al-Deen Al-Syowty, *Al-Atkon Fee Alom Al-Qur'an* [*The Perfection of Quranic Theology*], vol. 2, p. 37, and Al-Hafz Al Kalbbi, *Al-Tasshel Fi Aleolom Al Tanzel* [*The Easiest Revelation of Theology*].

CHAPTER 6: MISINFORMED BY THE MEDIA

1. Source obtained from the Internet: The transcript of *The Oprah Show* with Queen Rania of Jordan, aired October 10, 2001, as posted at the Oprah.com website on 12/26/01.
2. From the hadith recorded by Sahih Al-Bukhari.
3. Source obtained from the Internet: The transcript of *The Oprah Show* with Queen Rania of Jordan, aired October 10, 2001, as posted at the Oprah.com website on 12/26/01.
4. Jews believe the Dome of the Rock is built on the site of Solomon's Temple. Islam's holiest site is the Black Stone in Mecca, Saudi Arabia, and its second most holy site is the Mosque of the Prophet, where Muhammad is buried in Medina, Saudi Arabia.

CHAPTER 7: HUMAN RIGHTS UNDER ISLAM

1. Sayyid Qutb, *Social Justice in Islam*, revised edition, translated by John B. Hardie (Oneonta, NY: Islamic Publications International, 2000).
2. Source obtained from the Internet: "Naguib Mahfouz—a Short bio-pic," A Naguib Mahfouz page, www.lemmus.demon.co.uk/mahfouz.htm.
3. Dr. Farag Foda, *Terrorism* (N.p: 1993), pp. 13–14.
4. "The Right of Political Asylum for Muslim Renegades in Holland," *The Islamic World*, vol. 1679 (December 8, 2000).

CHAPTER 9: MUHAMMAD DECLARES JIHAD

1. Ibn Hisham, *Biography* [of Muhammad], vol. 2, pp. 448, 488; also Ibn Kathir, *Biography* [of Muhammad], vol. 22, pp. 100, 207. Ibn Hisham was an Islamic historian.
2. Ibn Hisham, vol. 4, p. 1527.
3. From the hadith recorded by al-Korashi, p. 59.
4. Ibn Hisham.
5. Ibid.
6. Dr. Solomon Basheer, *Tawazn al-Naka-ed* [*All the Unsimilar Things Are Equal*], p. 121.
7. Ebn Garir Al-Tobari, *The History of the Prophet and the Kings*, vol. 5, p. 27.
8. Al-Balezri, *Conquest of the Countries*, vol. 2 (publication information unknown), p. 310.
9. From the hadith recorded by Sahih Al-Bukhari.
10. Ibn Saad, *Al-Tabkat* [*The Layers*], vol. 3, p. 43.

CHAPTER 10: THE ULTIMATE GOAL OF JIHAD

1. All these quotes come from Mawlana Abul Ala Mawdudi, *Jihad in Islam* (India: 1970s).
2. Nabil Khalifa, *Lebanon and the Heart of the Islamic Revolution* (Beirut, 1984), pp. 93, 120.

CHAPTER 12: WHEN LIES ARE JUSTIFIED

1. Ibn Taymiyah, *Al-Sarim Almslowl alla Shatem Alrasool* [*The Sword on the Neck of the Accuser of Muhammad*], p. 221.
2. Al-Mansowry, *Al-taib Wal kabith* [*The Pure and the Unpure*], p. 199.
3. Ibn Kathir, *Al-Bedaia Wl-Nahaia* [*The Beginning and the End*] (Cairo, Egypt: Dar-al-maarif, 1962).
4. Ibid.
5. Egyptian president's national address after the first day of the Iraqi invasion of Kuwait.
6. The Quran refers to this incident in Surah 24:11, which speaks of "those who brought forth the slander."
7. Gazoli Saibin, *Ehia Al-owlom Al-Den* [*A Revival of the Religious Books*] (Cairo, Egypt: Maktabet al-Turas, 1971), pp. 3, 137.

CHAPTER 13: MUHAMMAD'S USE OF MOSQUES

1. Source obtained from the Internet: "U.S. Bombs Hit Mosque, Kills 15 Worshippers," Lebanon News Center at www.lebanon-guide.com (October 24, 2001).
2. William Branigin and Rajiv Chandrasekaran, "Informants Enable a Deadly Raid," *Washington Post* (October 25, 2001): Page A10.
3. Mahmoud Fouzi, *Abed Al-Halim Mousa* [*Secrets of the Resignation of Mohammed*], 2nd ed. (Cairo, Egypt: LFE Library French/Egyptian, n.d.), p. 40.

CHAPTER 14: FOREFATHERS OF TERRORISM

1. These three murders were recorded in a narrative by the Islamic historian Ebby Muhammad Abd El-Malak (son of Ebn-Hasham El-Matraffi), who died in Egypt in 835. This early Islamic history was never intended to be read by any foreigner or non-Muslim. I read this book in the library at Al-Azhar. I believe it may also be translated into English.
2. From the hadith recorded by Sahih Al-Bukhari, volume titled *Book of Jihad.*
3. Shahrstanni, *Religion and Sects* (Cairo, Egypt); p. 114, and Aby-El-Hassan Al-Ashri, *Islamic Articles*, vol. 1, p. 88.

CHAPTER 15: THE FOUNDING FATHER OF MODERN JIHAD

1. Adel Hamooda, *Sayyid Qutb: From the Village to the Gallows* (Cairo, Egypt: Sinai Publishing, 1987), pp. 92–94.
2. To my amazement, the English translation of one of Sayyid Qutb's books, *Social Justice in Islam*, is actually available at Amazon.com.
3. Sayyid Qutb, *Ma'alim fi el-Tareek* [*Signs Along the Road*] as quoted in Hamooda, *Sayyid Qutb.*
4. Ibid., p. 10.
5. Ibid., p. 22.
6. Ibid.
7. Ibid.

CHAPTER 16: THE PHILOSOPHERS OF JIHAD

1. As quoted in Salah Serea, "Clips of Message of Faith," *El-Yakaza El-*

Arabeya [*Arabic Revival Magazine*] (December 1986).
2. Ibid.
3. Ibid.
4. Shokri Moustafa, *El-Tawaseemat* [*Expectation*] (Cairo, Egypt: Shorouk International, n.d.).
5. *Rose El-Yousef Magazine* (July 11,1977): p. 6.
6. Shokri Moustafa, *Al-Kalafa* [*The Leader*] (Cairo, Egypt: Shorouk International, n.d.).

CHAPTER 19: TREACHERY BETWEEN TERRORISTS

1. Adel Hamooda, *Bombs and the Quran,* 3rd ed. (Cairo, Egypt: Sinai Publishing, 1989), p. 44.
2. That committee included Mohammed Abdul-Salam Farag, Abod Al-Zomor, Karm Zohdi, Najeh Ibrahim, Fouad Al-Dolabi, Ali Sharif, Essam Driya, Assim Abdul-Majed, Hamdi Abdul Rahman and Talat Qusam.
3. Following are the regions and their leaders: Cairo and Al-Giza region, Mohammed Abdul-Salam Farag; Al Minya region, Essam Driya and Fouad Al-Dolabi; Asyut region, Assim Abdul-Majed, Osama Hafez and Najeh Ibrahim; Quna and Nagh Hamadi regions, Ali Sharif and Talat Qusam.

CHAPTER 22: JIHAD BLEEDS OUT OF EGYPT

1. From the hadith recorded by Sahih al-Bukhari.

CHAPTER 23: NEW STRATEGY: ATTACK THE WEST

1. I received this information from a video produced by the United States Coptic Church association. The Coptic Church is the largest Christian denomination in Egypt. If you want more details, contact the director of the U.S. Copts association—Mike@copts.com.

CHAPTER 25: BRINGING THE GOSPEL TO MUSLIMS

1. Don Belt, "In Focus: World of Islam," *National Geographic Magazine* (January 2002): p. 79.

Glossary

Abbas al-Madani—leader and official spokesman of the Algerian Islamic Salvation Front

Ahmed Yassin—spiritual leader of the Palestinian Hamas

Al-Azhar University—oldest Islamic university in the world; spiritual authority of Islam located in Cairo, Egypt

al-Gama'a al-Islamiyya—the Islamic Group (IG); emerged during the 1970s mainly in Egyptian jails and later on in some of the Egyptian universities

al-Husayn—son of Ali ibn Abi Talib, cousin of Muhammad

Ali Belhadj—popular Algerian preacher who also served in leadership with the Algerian Islamic Salvation Front

Ali ibn Abi Talib—first cousin of Muhammad and one of his earliest converts; fourth caliph, selected as caliph after murder of Uthman; one of the Righteous Caliphs

al-Jihad—radical fundamentalist group established in Egypt that spread to many Muslim countries, such as Palestine and others

Allah—the God of Islam

al-Qaeda—fundamentalist Islamic organization led by Osama bin Laden

Anwar al-Sadat—former president of Egypt; assassinated by radical Muslim fundamentalists on October 6, 1981

Ayatollah Ruhollah Khomeini—chief Islamic leader of Iran from 1979 to 1989; returned to Iran in 1979 from exile in France after the shah fled Iran

ISLAM AND TERRORISM . . . .

Ayman al-Zawahiri—leader of the al-Jihad; on FBI's Most Wanted Terrorist list

Battle of Badr—First battle of Muhammad in which he defeated his rivals from Mecca at the Valley of Badr

Caliph—title given to those who succeeded the prophet Muhammad as real or nominal ruler of the Muslim world, with all his powers except that of prophecy; from the Arabic word *khalifa*, literally meaning "one who replaces someone else who left or died"

el Kharij—seventh-century Islamic movement calling for return to purity of faith

Gamal Abdel Nasser—president of Egypt, 1953–1970

George Habash—leader of the Popular Front for the Liberation of Palestine

hadith—the reported sayings and actions of Muhammad recorded in six sets of books

Hamas—Islamic Resistance Movement located in Palestine

Hasan al-Turabi—leader of the Sudanese fundamentalist Islamic organization al-Islamia

Hassan al-Banna—founder and first leader of the Muslim Brotherhood Movement; assassinated by Egyptian police in 1949

Hassan Nasrallah—Hizbollah leader

hijab—a woman's veil or head scarf

Hizbollah (also Hezbollah)—"Party of God"; Lebanese Islamic party

Hosni Mubarak—Egyptian president; assumed office after assassination of Anwar al-Sadat

Ibn Hisham—early Islamic historian

Ibn Taymiyah—thirteenth- and fourteenth-century scholar who called for a return to the ways of the "pious ancestors" (*al-salaf al-salih*)

imam—an Islamic leader; usually in charge of a mosque

infidel—one who rejects the teachings of Islam

Islamic Salvation Front (FIS)—North Africa's first legal Islamic political party, first recognized by Algeria's government in 1988; later split into a moderate group and a more militant wing called the Islamic Salvation Army

Jamaat-i-Islami (Islamic Society)—fundamentalist Islamic organization of Pakistan

jihad—holy war; fighting those who resist Islam

jizyah—tax that must be paid by anyone who chooses to keep their own faith and not convert to Islam

Khaled al-Islambouli—one of the convicted assassins of Egyptian president Anwar al-Sadat

Mahmoud Nokrashy Pasha—premier of Egypt assassinated by Muslim Brotherhood on December 28, 1948

Mawlana Abul Ala Mawdudi—leader of the Jamaat-i-Islami of Pakistan

Mecca—Birthplace of Muhammad and place where he first received Quranic verses from the angel Gabriel. Located in present-day Saudi Arabia.

Medina—originally called Yathrib; name of city was changed to Medina ("the Prophet's city") after Muhammad relocated there. Located in present-day Saudi Arabia.

Muammar Qaddafi—Libyan leader

Muawiya ibn Abi Sufyan—governor of Syria who opposed the selection of Ali as caliph after the murder of Uthman

Muhammad ibn Abd al-Wahhab—founder of the 18th century puritanical Wahhabi movement

Muhammad Reza Shah Pahlavi—shah of Iran at the time of the revolution led by Ayatollah Khomeini in 1979

Muhammad—Arab prophet and founder of Islam, born A.D. 570. The Westernized spelling is Mohammed.

Muslim Brotherhood—Islamic organization encompassing several nations and Islamic groups

Mustafa Kemal Ataturk—Turkish leader who abolished the Ottoman/Turkish caliphate system in 1922

Naguib Mahfouz—winner of the 1988 Nobel Prize for Literature; stabbed outside of his home in Cairo in 1994

naskh—system of Quranic interpretation where new verses override previous verses

Omar Abdel Rahman—former leader of al-Jihad in Egypt, currently imprisoned in the United States for his involvement in the 1993 World Trade Center bombing

Osama bin Laden—suspected mastermind of the September 11, 2001 terrorist attacks against the United States; leader of al-Qaeda; on FBI's Most Wanted Terrorist list

People of the Book—Jews and Christians, so named in the Quran

Popular Front for the Liberation of Palestine—progressive working-class party of Palestine, guided by Marxism and Leninism

Quran—the Islamic holy book

Quraysh—powerful governing tribe of Mecca at the time of Muhammad's birth; Muhammad's father, a trader named Abdullah, was a member of this tribe.

Ramadan—the ninth month of the Muslim calendar, during which a daily fast is observed from dawn until sunset

Saddam Hussein—Iraqi political leader, president since 1979

Salman Rushdie—Writer of *The Satanic Verses,* which caused the Ayatollah Khomeini to issue a *fatwa* (legal opinion) sanctioning his death

Sayyid Qutb—Egyptian author and philosopher whose writings were banned by Egyptian government; he was arrested and sentenced to death in 1965, executed in 1966

Sharia—Islamic law regarding the duties of Muslims toward Allah

sheikh—term of reverence for an ordained religious leader in Islam

Shiite—Islamic sect; followers of Ali ibn Abi Talib as the successor of Muhammad

Shokri Ahmad Moustafa—popular Islamic movement leader in Egypt. Executed by the government in 1977.

Sunni—Islamic sect; followers of Umar ibn al-Khattab as the successor of Muhammad

Surah—a chapter of the Quran

Taliban—Islamic fundamentalist group of Afghanistan

Uhud—hill where famous battle was fought by Muhammad and his new converts against Arabs who rejected the call of Islam

Umar ibn al-Khattab—second caliph assassinated in A.D. 644 by a Persian slave bent on avenging the conquest of his people

Uthman ibn Affan—third leader of Islam

Wahhabi—18th century puritanical movement that in time became the official creed of the Saudi dynasty; adherents observed literalism and strict observance of Muslim rituals

Yasser Arafat—chairman of the Palestine Liberation Organization (PLO)

Yathrib—ancient name of the city of Medina; name changed to Medina ("the Prophet's city") after Muhammad relocated there

Yazid—son of Muawiya ibn Abi Sufyan

Bibliography

BOOKS PUBLISHED IN ARABIC

Abdul-Majed, Assim and Najeh Ibrahim. *Al-Jamatuleslamiah* [*The Constitution of the Islamic Jihad*]. (The authors wrote this book while in prison.)

Al-Banna, Hassan. *Wednesday Dialogue*, mid-1900s.

Al-Masry, Ebn Eyas. *Al-Nejum Al-Zaharah* [*The Bright Stars*].

Al-Nadawy, Abu al-Hasan. *The Struggle Between Eastern and Western Ideology*. (Originally published in India and then published in Egypt.)

Al-Salem, Mohammed Abed. *Al-Fareda Al-Gaaba* [*The Missing Commitments*].

Al-Tobari, Ebn Garir. *The History of the Prophet and the Kings*. (This is the oldest Islamic history book.)

Commentaries on the Quran written by the following authors: Al-Alussi, Ibn Kathir, Al-Zamakshary, Al-Bidawy. All published by Almoktar al-Islami in Cairo, Egypt.

El-Rahman, Aisha Abd. *The Wives of the Prophet*. Morocco: Dar El Hilal, 1971.

Foda, Farag. *Terrorism*. N.p., 1993.

The Hadith (six series of books) published by Almoktar al-Islami, Cairo, Egypt. The authors of these book series include: Sahih al-Bukhari and al-Korashi.

Hamooda, Adel. *Sayyid Qutb: From the Village to the Gallows*. Cairo, Egypt: Sinai Publishing, 1987. (Hamooda is an

Egyptian author who specializes in books about Islamic terrorism.)

——. *The Road to Violence* (a book about Shokri Moustafa). Cairo, Egypt: Sinai Publishing, 1987.

——. *Bombs and the Quran: The Story of Jihad Fundamentalist Groups.* Cairo, Egypt: Sinai Publishing, 1989.

Huwaody, Fahmi. *Hata la-Takon-Fitnah* [*Preventing Conflict*], 2nd ed. Cairo, Egypt: Dar el-Shorouk, 1989.

Ibn Taymiyah. *The Greatest Fatwa.*

Imara, Mohammed. *Mawdudi and the Islamic Revival.* Cairo, Egypt: Dar el-Shorouk, 1987.

Mawdudi, Mawlana Abul Ala. *The Islamic Government.* Cairo, Egypt, 1980.

Moustafa, Shokri. *Al-Kalafa* [*The Leader*].

Qutb, Mohamed. *Are We Muslims?*

Qutb, Sayyid. *In the Shadow of the Quran* (a commentary on the Quran). Cairo, Egypt and Beirut, Lebanon: Dar el-Shorouk International.

——. *Signs Along the Road.* Cairo, Egypt and Beirut, Lebanon: Dar el-Shorouk International.

——. *This Religion.* Cairo, Egypt and Beirut, Lebanon: Dar el-Shorouk International.

——. *Social Justice in Islam.* Cairo, Egypt and Beirut, Lebanon: Dar el-Shorouk International.

——. *The Picture of Arts in the Quran.* Cairo, Egypt and Beirut, Lebanon: Dar el-Shorouk International.

——. *Our War With the Jews.* Cairo, Egypt and Beirut, Lebanon: Dar el-Shorouk International.

——. *The Future of This Religion.* Cairo, Egypt and Beirut, Lebanon: Dar el-Shorouk International.

——. *Establishing Islamic Society.* Cairo, Egypt and Beirut, Lebanon: Dar el-Shorouk International.

Serea, Salah. *El-Tawaseemat* [*Expectation*].

Shalaby, Ahmed. *The Islamic Encyclopedia*, Cairo edition.

——. *The Encyclopedia of Islamic Civilization*, Cairo edition.

——. *Islam and the World.*

——. *The War in Kuwait.*

——. *The Jews in Darkness.*

BOOKS PUBLISHED IN ENGLISH

Arnold, Thomas. *The Preaching of Islam.* Columbia, MO: South Asia Books, 1990.

——. *The Caliphate.* New York: Oxford Press, 2000.

Bodansky, Yossef. *Target America: Terrorism in the USA Today.* New York: S.P.I. Books/Shapolsky Publishers, Inc., 1993.

Emerton, Ephraim. *Medieval Europe.* No publishing information available.

Hadi, Abdul. *The Cross and the Crescent.* No publishing information available.

Hitti, Philip. *The Arabs: A Short History.* Washington, DC: Regnery Publishing, Inc., 1996.

Huntington, Samuel. *The Clash of Civilizations and the Remaking of World Order.* Touchstone Books, 1998.

Nixon, Richard. *Seize the Moment: America's Challenge in a One-Superpower World.* New York: Simon and Schuster, 1992.

Sarton, George. *A History of Science.* New York: Norton and Company, 1952.

RECOMMENDED READING

Morey, Robert A. *Islamic Invasion*. Las Vegas, NV: Christian Scholar's Press, 2001.

——. *Winning The War Against Radical Islam*. Las Vegas, NV: Christian Scholar's Press, 2002.

Shorrosh, A. *Islam Revealed*. Nashville, TN: Thomas Nelson, 1988.

Other Books by the Author

Islam and the Jews (Charisma House, 2003)—An
overview why Muslims literally hate the Jews and why
Muslims believe Islam is the perfection and completion
of Judaism and Christianty

For information about having Dr. Mark Gabriel speak at
your church, conference or school, contact:

Hope for the Nations
Mark A. Gabriel
P. O. Box 181974
Casselberry, FL 32718-1974